The MONOCLE
Travel Guide Series

29

Barcelona

For more information, please visit *gestalten.com*

Bibliographic information published by the Deutsche Nationalbibliothek: The Deutsche Nationalbibliothek lists this publication in the Deutsche Nationalbibliografie; detailed bibliographic data are available online at *dnb.d-nb.de*

Monocle editor in chief and chairman: *Tyler Brûlé*
Monocle editor: *Andrew Tuck*
Books editor: *Joe Pickard*
Guide editor: *Melkon Charchoglyan*

Designed by *Monocle*
Proofreading by *Monocle*
Typeset in *Plantin & Helvetica*

Printed by *Offsetdruckerei Grammlich, Pliezhausen*

Made in Germany

Published by *Gestalten*, Berlin 2018
ISBN 978-3-89955-945-3

© Die Gestalten Verlag GmbH & Co. KG, Berlin 2018

Welcome
—— Barcelona
but different

You could say that Barcelona is too famous for its own good: a reputation for *tapas*, *football* and *raucous parties* in the Barri Gòtic attracts blinkered visitors by the busload. But there's much more to Barna – as it's affectionately known – than *sangria in the sun*.

A few steps beyond the well-trodden alleyways of the Ciutat Vella (Old Town) lies an elegant city with a unique character (not to mention language), strong *civic pride* and *inimitable culture*. In the 19th century it was a rapidly modernising metropolis – and the most prosperous in Spain. With the leaps of progress came wealth and a licence for creativity; architects such as *Antoni Gaudí* raised *dreamlike structures* that forever shaped both the look and feel of the cityscape.

The 20th century brought a heavy dose of suffering, first under the Spanish civil war and then the Franco dictatorship. But Barcelona refused to buckle and instead placed itself firmly on the map as a centre of business, fashion and design, with creative minds from *Joan Miró* to *Ricardo Bofill* maintaining its reputation as a factory for innovative ideas. The century ended on a high: the 1992 Olympic Games brought a new era of prosperity that paved the way for the joyful, confident and liveable city you'll find today.

Join us for an inclusive yet intimate amble through Barcelona's well-stocked independent shops, eminent fashion houses, forward-thinking museums and first-rate restaurants, as well as a round-up of the best bars to while away an afternoon with a glass of *vermut*. *Salut!* — (M)

Contents
—— Navigating the city

Use the key below to help navigate the guide section by section.

 H Hotels

 F Food and drink

 R Retail

 T Things we'd buy

 E Essays

C Culture

D Design and architecture

S Sport and fitness

W Walks

Barcelona
—— A city in two parts

Seen from above, Barcelona is a tale of two cities. In the centre you'll find Ciutat Vella (Old Town), which extends from Plaça de Catalunya to the waterfront. Its three medieval neighbourhoods – El Raval, Barri Gòtic and El Born – form the city's beating heart, packed with restaurants, bars, shops, museums and, inevitably, tourists.

When Madrid granted the city permission to remove the old city walls in 1854, Barcelona began to grow at an unprecedented rate. The new areas – notably Eixample (Expansion) to the north, Poblenou (New Town) to the east and Sant Antoni to the south – are where you'll find the most sought-after tables, the best art galleries and most of the *modernista* architecture.

For an even more authentic flavour there's Gràcia to the far north: a standalone town absorbed by the city in the 19th century. To the south of Sant Antoni is Poble-sec, with its flourishing food scene, and towering above it all is Montjuïc: this mountain was the epicentre of the 1992 Olympics and hosts many museums, as well as idyllic spots for a picnic.

↗ Sant Andreu

LA SAGRERA

NAVAS

GUINARDÓ

SANT MARTÍ DE PROVENÇALS

BAIX GUINARDÓ

● Recinte Modernista de Sant Pau

EL CLOT

PROVENÇALS DEL POBLENOU

EL CAMP DE L'ARPA DEL CLOT

FRONT MARÍTIM

ÀCIA

SAGRADA FAMILIA

La Sagrada Familia

Torre Glòries

Parc del Fòrum ↗

FORT PIENC

POBLENOU

Platja de la Mar Bella ●

Casa Milà

DRETA DE L'EIXAMPLE

Passeig de Sant Joan

Passeig de Gràcia

Gran Via de les Corts Catalanes

BOGATELL

Casa Batlló ●

d'Aragó ●

VILA OLÍMPICA

Arc de Triomf

Plaça de Catalunya ●

Palau de la Música Catalana

● Mercat de Santa Caterina

Parc de la Ciutadella

● Museu Picasso

Peix Olímpic Frank Gehry

MACBA ●

EL BORN

BARCELONETA

EL RAVAL

Catedral de Barcelona

BARRI GÒTIC

Platja de la ● Barceloneta

SANT NTONI

POBLE-SEC

Monument a Cristòfor Colom

ación Joan Miró

MONTJUÏC

● Castell de Montjuïc

0   500M   N

Need to know
—— Barcelona back to basics

Independence
Sensitive subject

The longstanding issue of Catalan independence and the formation of the Republic of Catalonia has undoubtedly reached defining moments in the recent past. But as a visitor there's little to fear from the sporadic and generally good-natured demonstrations organised by both sides. Plus they're easy to avoid, with marches publicised well in advance.

An element of measure will be required when entering into a conversation with someone of either persuasion. As you can imagine, it's a heated subject that has the potential to quickly lead to huffs and gesticulation.

Tipping
Keep your change

In general, tipping is rarely expected but a good rule to follow is to do as you would at home. If the food and service are to your liking in a restaurant, it's a welcome gesture to leave a 10 to 15 per cent gratuity. Taxis don't expect tips and it's common to find yourself facing a bewildered driver if you try to leave one.

Language lessons
Words on the street

Many wonder whether there's much of a difference between the Spanish language (Castilian) and Catalan – and are subsequently surprised to learn that the answer is yes. Many Catalans are so protective of their identity and language that they won't switch to Castilian. While Spanish speakers should still get the gist, it's worth learning a few Catalan phrases to lighten the mood. If you're lucky you may even receive a smile for your efforts.

Opening hours
Take your time

Lots of independent shops in the city adhere to opening hours that the rest of the world might view as commercial suicide. While no one actually nips home for a siesta, small shops typically close for lunch between 13.00 and 16.00. However, larger shops and multinational outlets stay open all day. Opening hours on the whole are a leisurely 10.00 to 20.00 or 21.00. Most retail offerings close on Sundays.

Just soaking up some rays on our long lunch break

Saints' days
Party people

Spain is renowned for frequently dropping everything and celebrating one saint or another with a bank holiday or, at the very least, a gathering of family and friends. Catalonia counts three days of its own in the mix, including that of Barcelona's patron saint, Sant Jordi (Saint George). On said day men buy women roses and women present men with a book. The entire city comes to a joyous standstill on 23 April as the *carrers* (streets) fill with book stalls and rose merchants.

Catalans also take to the streets on 11 September, a day for remembering the fall of the sovereign Principality of Catalonia in 1714. Meanwhile the celebration of Sant Esteve on Boxing Day is a chance to reuse leftovers in cannelloni, the ideal hangover cure after a boozy Christmas.

Etiquette
Meet and greet

Barcelonans are a warm and friendly bunch. When meeting someone for the first time or simply saying hello, it's two kisses (a simple handshake will suffice between men). Once the pleasantries are over there are few hidden rules of etiquette to consider during any tête-à-tête with a resident. Speaking with passion and a touch of volume is welcome, as is a friendly pat on the arm or back. Just avoid saying anything positive when it comes to Real Madrid (*see page 87*).

Dress code
Under-exposure

For those who spend most of their lives in the higher reaches of the northern hemisphere it may be tempting to dig out the shorts and flip-flops when temperatures teeter into double figures. But there's no bigger indication of a *guiri* (slang for foreigner) than the sight of a pair of milk bottles mooching down La Rambla.

By all means do as you please but you won't find Barcelonans in shorts between October and April. On warmer winter days it's better to stick to trousers and rolled-up shirt sleeves.

Food and drink
A city to savour

Barcelona is quite simply the land of milk and honey for food fanatics. The Catalan capital is packed with cafés, bars, restaurants, delis, ice-cream parlours, patisseries, wine shops and markets. Plus there are all manner of specialist culinary producers to suit any preference, from gourmets and gourmands to picky eaters and shallow pockets.

A crash course in Catalan cuisine is best undertaken at one of the city's many food markets, where stalls offer complimentary tasters and corner bars whip up simple delicacies with fresh daily produce supplied by stands within a stone's throw of the chef. When eating out remember that dinner at 22.00 or later is the norm – anything before 20.00 is sacrilege.

Barna vs Barça
To the letter

There's one mistake that the majority of visitors to the city make time and time again and you'll see locals wince ever so slightly every time it happens. Even those with a good knowledge of the culture often fail to make the distinction: Barça is the nickname for FC Barcelona, while Barna is the diminutive for the city. "I'm flying to Barna to watch Barça." Got it?

There's no mistaking the Olympic Stadium

Sporting city
Everyone's a winner

Since the Olympics in 1992, Barcelona has been widely recognised as the host city to have most benefited from the Games, with a legacy plan that transformed the entire urban fabric to the advantage of the population. Beyond its infrastructure improvements the city's sporting legacy includes a wide range of Olympic-quality facilities, myriad opportunities to practise sports in the open air and a booming sports-conference industry. It's also home to a long list of global sports and outerwear brands.

Our top picks:

01 **Nømad Coffee:** Barcelona's superlative coffee, roasted in Poblenou. *see page 43*

02 **Casa Atlântica:** Colourful Mediterranean ceramics and homeware. *see page 57*

03 **Entrepanes Díaz:** Hearty lunch fare in an old-school bar. *see page 36*

04 **Barcelona Pavilion:** Mies Van der Rohe's modernist marvel. *see page 109*

05 **Museu Picasso:** One of the world's finest collections of the artist's works. *see pages 96*

06 **Santa Eulalia:** The city's most elegant and esteemed fashion retailer. *see page 51*

07 **Sala Parés:** Spain's oldest commercial gallery. *see pages 99*

08 **Iriarte Iriarte:** Bespoke leather goods that are worth the wait. *see pages 61*

09 **Casa Vicens:** Antoni Gaudí's polychrome wonder of a building. *see page 111*

10 **La Dama:** Catalan and French cuisine meet in a *modernista* space. *see page 34*

My favourite is the Magic Fountain of Montjuïc!

Hotels
— Go to
your room

Barcelona has been all too successful in tempting tourists and today there remains a surfeit of shoddy hostels and overpriced pensions to house them all. However, a decision to limit the number of new hotels has stemmed the overdevelopment and allowed the cream of the hospitality crop some space to grow. As you'll see, the city has more than its share of leafy rooftops on which to recline and older buildings to repurpose – and plenty of heads to vie for the beds.

Our rundown errs on the side of the independents, with a few interesting bigger-brand inclusions where the space warrants it. Expect sea-facing suites, off-the-main-drag dorms and gothic boltholes galore. Too much choice is overrated so we've bounced up and down on the best beds in town in order to recommend the finest places in which to park yourself. *De res*.

① Soho House Barcelona,
Barri Gòtic
Join the club

The UK-based hospitality
firm Soho House & Co
expanded into Barcelona in
2016. The on-point conversion
of this residential building is a
high watermark of hospitality,
where original mosaic and
parquet floors give way to
vaulted red-brick ceilings
(common in Catalonia).

The downstairs restaurant
Cecconi's does a brisk trade
in Venetian dishes, while the
rooftop offers an enviable view
towards the Port Vell marina
and the sea beyond. The usual
trappings are available to
members, from an old-school
gym to a 36-seat cinema and
a horseshoe-shaped terrazzo
bar on the fifth floor. The 57
rooms – available for non-
members to book – feature
a tasteful mix of found and
bought furniture, with Bakelite
telephones, his-and-hers sinks,
Roberts radios and well-
stocked minibars.
*4 Plaça del Duc de Medinaceli,
08002
+34 93 220 4600
sohohousebarcelona.com*

MONOCLE COMMENT: Plaça del
Duc de Medinaceli, where the
club and hotel entrance lies, is
the setting for a scene in Pedro
Almodóvar's 1999 film *Todo
sobre mi madre.*

2

Hotel Pulitzer,
Dreta de l'Eixample
Prize property

Sit in the lobby and watch the
dapper clientele clip across
the parquet floors to get a
sense of what the Pulitzer
does best: attract a decent
crowd. It opened in 2004 and
a 2017 revamp by interior
designer Lázaro Rosa-Violán
has done wonders to lift the
place, keeping the media set
resolutely sated and seated.

The 50-cover Greenhouse
restaurant – run by chef
Damien Bolger, who trained
in California and France
– ensures a steady flow of
rumbling tums. Meanwhile
a fleet of Brompton bicycles
stands by the door to whisk
customers around the city.
8 Carrer de Bergara, 08002
+34 93 481 6767
hotelpulitzer.es

MONOCLE COMMENT: Despite
its location near La Rambla,
the Pulitzer is never overrun
– although the rooftop bar is
always busy at the weekend.

③
Margot House,
Dreta de l'Eixample
Little house on the passeig

Slap bang in Eixample's
frenetic Passeig de Gràcia,
up a single flight of stairs in
an otherwise unremarkable
building, is perhaps the city's
most surprising stopover. With
just nine rooms, Margot House
(pronounce the "t") is small
but comfy, replete with wooden
finishes and just-so interiors:
think Hans J Wegner chairs,
Santa & Cole floor lamps and
a plentiful library.

The well-appointed public
space, consisting of an open
dining room and kitchen, is
more Nordic than Catalan.
Triple-glazed windows and
blackout blinds help create a
feeling of welcome seclusion.
46 Passeig de Gràcia, 08007
+34 93 272 0076
margothouse.es

MONOCLE COMMENT: Tasteful
details such as personalised
messages scrawled on the
cupboard mirrors add a human
touch to the pristine surrounds.

④
Casa Bonay, Dreta de l'Eixample
Talk of the town

"There are so many hotels with a coffeeshop, bar and restaurant," says Inés Miró-Sans (*see page 91*), a young entrepreneur who opened this 67-room stopover in early 2016. "But this is a place for *me* to learn and collaborate." She gestures towards Satan's Coffee Corner, a concrete-floored, timber-tabled café that shares the ground floor with the lively Libertine restaurant, a small bookshop, a forest of banana plants and a steady mix of guests and locals.

In the hotel part of the converted 1869 townhouse, original mosaic floors and terracotta tiles have been spruced up by the talented folk at Brooklyn-based interior firm Studio Tack. The guest rooms are capacious – with Teixidors throws (*see page 68*), spare-but-smart wooden decor and a teeming mini-bar – and the outdoor showers in the terrace rooms are a refreshing touch.
700 Gran Via de les Corts Catalanes, 08010
+34 93 545 8050
casabonay.com

MONOCLE COMMENT: Elephant, Crocodile, Monkey is excellent for Thai food, while rooftop bar Chiringuito has tasty tapas and Spanish wine.

(5)
Hotel Brummell, Poble-sec
Concrete jungle

Located in an enviable spot
between the city, sea and
mountains, Brummell is
a seemly 20-room affair
that's (fairly) central but
feels a world away from
the touristy throng. Rusted
tables and concrete walls
sit alongside frondy plants
and an edible garden.

Owner Christian Schallert
fell in love with the then
derelict building back in 2015
and challenged architect Inma
Rábano to fix it up. He also
commissioned design duo
Blankslate (famed in these
parts for the Federal Café in
El Raval) to give a tropical
modern twist to the Catalan
backdrop. Rooms are bijou
but views are vast and if you
book a penthouse (there are
two) you can expect your
own alfresco bathtub.
174 Nou de la Rambla, 08004
+34 93 125 8622
hotelbrummell.com

MONOCLE COMMENT: Pack a
picnic in your complementary
Brummell cotton tote and
scamper up Montjuïc to
discover why they call it
Magic Mountain.

❻

The Wittmore, Barri Gòtic
Little Britain

Designed with a fictitious, portly and pork-chopped patron called Lord Nicholas Wittmore in mind (his portrait hangs in the lobby, complete with a raffishly off-kilter bow tie), this tucked-away 22-room bolthole has an unexpectedly British feel. The lobby is all sink-in red sofas, tartan turns and a library that gives way to a small central courtyard and green wall bursting with verdant plants.

Some details – such as the open fire – are a little kitsch but overall the feel is comfy, and finishes from proprietor Narcís Barceló are well-chosen and tasteful. The reception hosts a substantial ebony desk, red curtains and brushed-brass pigeon holes, while the rooms are homely and accommodating.

7 Carrer de Riudarenes, 08002
+34 93 550 0885
thewittmore.com

MONOCLE COMMENT: In-room amenities include full-size bottles of Scotch, toiletries from DR Harris & Co and Proraso shaving cream from Italy.

(7)

Alma Barcelona, Dreta
de l'Eixample
Smart stopover

Joaquín Ausejo has been
courting a discerning clientele
since he opened Alma in
2011. On a street just off busy
Passeig de Gràcia, the dusky-
hued hotel – clad in wood,
leather and metal accents – was
once the nondescript office of
a pharmaceutical firm and the
courtyard garden was rescued
from the ignominious fate
of being a carpark. The feel
is urban and urbane, while
the downstairs restaurant –
presided over by chef Gio
Esteve – turns out fine food
to in-the-know locals.
271 Carrer de Mallorca, 08008
+34 93 216 4490
almabarcelona.com

MONOCLE COMMENT: This
72-room hotel has cracked
a tough formula: it attracts
both arty types and business-
minded Barcelonans.

This is the life...

Ⓘ
Cotton House Hotel,
Dreta de l'Eixample
Cut from a fine cloth

The story of this 19th-
century building is told in
two staircases: to the right as
you enter through the stately
wooden doors is the original
white-marble affair, while on
the left is a contemporary
spiral model suspended from
six floors above – a feature of a
1957 refit. Both lead to a bright
first-floor reception, the Batuar
bar and restaurant, and a vast
terrace by Barcelona design
go-to Lázaro Rosa-Violán.

Opened in 2015 as a
Marriott hotel, the building
was once home to a family who
plied their trade in textiles, a
fact referenced in the hotel's
bespoke shirt-tailoring space
L'Atelier. The 83 rooms range
from minuscule to massive.
670 Gran Via de les Corts
Catalanes, 08010
+34 93 450 5045
hotelcottonhouse.com

MONOCLE COMMENT: A big-
brand-but-beautiful renovation,
with grand communal areas and
a lively bar and terrace (which
regularly hosts a craft market),
breathed new life into the hotel.
Be sure to explore every nook.

Ⓗ
Mercer Hotel Barcelona,
Barri Gòtic
On the ramparts

Made up of original Roman-
era walls and 14th-century
pointed archways, this
atmospheric 28-room affair
is located down a steep street
in Barri Gòtic. The peculiar
architectural history means
that no two rooms are the
same; many boast original
exposed bricks and wooden
ceiling struts alongside Italian
furniture and the odd tasteful
Arne Jacobsen lamp here
or Carl Hansen & Søn chair
there. The light is better the
higher you climb up the three-
storey building; proximity to
the central courtyard also helps
in this regard.
7 Carrer dels Lledó, 08002
+34 93 310 7480
mercerbarcelona.com

MONOCLE COMMENT:
Downstairs the eponymous
restaurant turns out a tidy
choice of Catalan cuisine
(try the grilled mussels), while
the small library, cocktail bar
and lobby overlooking the
courtyard are all apt places
to linger with a *vermut*.

10

The Serras Hotel Barcelona, Barri Gòtic
Work of art

Set back from the road facing the Port Vell marina and out to sea, this waterfront hotel has a laidback tone set by the subtle high hats of the background jazz playing in the airy lobby. "We didn't want to be black and white and modern, nor just a classic hotel," says general manager Antonio Bignone. "Instead we tried to play with wooden textures and Mediterranean colours."

The result is an artful accomplishment, with interiors by designer Eva Martínez and vast beds kitted out with comfortable Hypnos mattresses. The downstairs restaurant is run by Marc Gascons and prepped in an open kitchen overseen by a quiet mezzanine.
9 Passeig de Colom, 08002
+34 93 169 1868
hoteltheserrasbarcelona.com

MONOCLE COMMENT: The 1846 façade was designed by Francesc Daniel Molina. And it met with approval: Pablo Picasso lived in the building for about a year from 1896.

Ogle-worthy architecture

01 **Mandarin Oriental, Dreta de l'Eixample:** You need only venture as far as the entrance ramp on Passeig de Gràcia (and gawp at the soaring five-storey atrium specked with irregular windows) to know that no expense was spared in the renovation of this 120-room hotel in a 1930s bank building.
mandarinoriental.com

02 **El Palauet Living, Gràcia:** Opened in 2010, this former private home (the name means "little palace") is dominated by an original oak staircase. It's replete with period features too: many-hued glass windows, parquet floors and a vast chandelier from 1906.
elpalauet.com

03 **Gran Hotel La Florida, Tibidabo:** Perched on Mount Tibidabo, a 20-minute drive from the city centre, this 70-room art deco gem has a lobby of iron, dusky wood and sculptures that waver between tasteful and ostentatious. Visit Café 1924 for a look but plump for a hotel closer to the action.
hotellaflorida.com

Back in play

The massive 500-room Hotel Princesa Sofia tower near Camp Nou (FC Barcelona's football stadium) has had a thoughtful revamp and is popular with the business crowd.
sofiabarcelona.com

Food and drink
—— Barcelona's best bites

Barcelona's microcosm of old and new cuisines exists within the context of Catalonia, a region with a food identity as fiercely defended as the local language, culture, history and football club. However, you'll also find food and wine from all corners of Spain and beyond, as well as modern restaurants improvising on time-honoured Catalan classics. Cured meat, cheese and fresh seafood are just some of the plentiful specialities, while the growing aperitivo trend will have you searching for a bottle of *vermut* before you know it.

It's a place of rules and traditions, of course: don't order fresh fish on a Monday (the best catch comes later in the week) and dinner before 20.00 is a faux pas. But beyond a few do's and don'ts, Barcelona is a city where the wine flows freely and wiping your plate clean with a hunk of bread isn't just accepted, it's actively encouraged. So embrace the gastronomic landscape, whether you're booking a sought-after table at the new hotspot or having a drawn-out evening at a family-run favourite. *Bon profit!*

Restaurants
Essential reservations

①
Xemei, Poble-sec
A taste of Venice

Don't expect much meat at Xemei. Serving Venetian food since 2006, here it's all about the fruits of the sea, including a tasty squid-ink spaghetti.

Gregarious twins Stefano and Max Colombo (*pictured, Max on left*) have carved a niche for themselves on the city's food scene. They leave a lasting impression, much like their intimate dining room with its eclectic mementos, well-worn furniture and organic wine that will keep you talking late into the night.
85 Passeig de l'Exposició, 08004
+34 93 553 5140
xemei.es

Joint effort
The furniture is as pleasing as the food on the plates

2

Mediamanga, L'Antiga Esquerra de l'Eixample
Modern classics

Instantly inviting with its art deco and modernist design accents, the narrow dining room of Mediamanga segues seamlessly into its open kitchen. Here chef Domenico Ungaro delicately plates up servings of fig carpaccio with shaved foie gras or seared red mullet with apricot emulsion.

Ungaro's focus is on raw ingredients of superlative quality and traditional recipes prepared simply but always with an added twist or technique. The resulting dishes are on a level of modernity in keeping with the tasteful decor courtesy of Barcelona designer Cristina Carulla.

13 Carrer d'Aribau, 08011
+ 34 93 832 5694
mediamanga.es

③
Els Pescadors, Poblenou
Seafood tradition

The sun-filled, whitewashed Plaça de Prim is populated by three ancient ombu trees, the last remaining 19th-century homes in the seaside fishermen's neighbourhood of Poblenou and, most importantly, the shady terrace of Els Pescadors.

In keeping with the tranquil square's maritime tradition, Els Pescadors has been serving super but simple roast fish, seafood stews and rice dishes since 1980. The terrace is a perfect spot to enjoy a leisurely lunch while the worn, marble tabletops and dark wooden trim of the welcoming dining room hark back to another era.
1 Plaça de Prim, 08005
+34 93 225 2018
elspescadors.com

④
Lomo Alto, Dreta de l'Eixample
Claim your steak

Lomo Alto has become the best steakhouse in Barcelona, perhaps even all of Spain. Known for *carne de buey* (mature oxen) and *vaca vieja* (former dairy cows), all its meat is hand-selected and matured in custom refrigerators. A dry-ageing process of 20 days to 12 months creates buttery-soft and intensely flavourful cuts.

The waiters are sommeliers for meat, describing the nuance of each cut and breed before carving your charcoal-grilled steaks tableside.
283-285 Carrer d'Aragó, 08009
+34 93 519 3000
lomoalto.barcelona

⑤
Kak Koy, Barri Gòtic
Expert Japanese

Barcelona loves Japanese food (mainly sushi) but while many of the city's options lack any discerning individuality, Kak Koy is in a league of its own.

Chef Hideki Matsuhisa's goal was to open a younger, more accessible locale of equal quality to his Michelin-starred Koy Shunka and Japanese tavern Shunka – and he's certainly hit the mark. Kak Koy is relaxed, with communal tables and a carefully selected menu of small dishes, many prepared on a traditional *robata* (charcoal grill).
16 Carrer de Ripoll, 08002
+34 93 302 8414
koyshunka.com

⑥

Elsa y Fred, El Born
Destination dining

The influences behind the design and menu at this petite gastrobar are far-reaching. The varied tastes and personal style of Catalan chef Ramón Miracle and Argentinian sisters and co-founders Camila and Sofia Matarazzo have resulted in a mix of small plates that know no borders, from ponzu and jalapeño to Spanish mackerel and pastrami.

With decor inspired by 1950s Europe, including a tiny terrace complete with hand-scrawled chalkboard menus, Elsa y Fred is always buzzing. From breakfast, brunch and lunch to post-work dinner and late-night drinks, the intimate bistro gives as much weight to its ambience as its food.

11 Carrer del Rec Comtal, 08003
+34 93 501 6611
elsayfred.es

⑦

Can Maño, Barceloneta
Simply delicious

Sometimes the best plan is to rub elbows with some locals and tuck into delicious authentic food without the glitz. A meal at Can Maño is a simple affair of grilled and fried fish and seafood – so simple, in fact, that the tender grilled squid comes with just lemon and parsley. The ultra-fresh seafood needs little garnish, however, and the atmosphere is lively. The house white is crisp, cold and so affordable that you could easily mistake the bottle price for that of a glass.

12 Carrer del Baluard, 08003
+34 93 319 3082

Must-try
Paella from Xiringuito Escribà, Poblenou
Originally from Valencia, paella is an integral part of traditional meals in Barcelona, where it's strictly lunchtime fare (to give your body all afternoon to digest) and best enjoyed by the beach. For a classic seafood paella, Xiringuito Escribà on Platja del Bogatell is one of the best in the city.
xiringuitoescriba.com

Suculent, El Raval
Soul food with style

The snout-to-tail cooking at Suculent – a restaurant designed in the style of an old-fashioned cellar – blends Catalan soul food with a healthy dose of good presentation. The vibe is casual, inviting and unpretentious; people don't come here to be seen, they come here to eat well.

The name is a play on the Catalan term *sucar lent* (to dip slowly), advice that any diner would be wise to follow when presented with a plate of salt-and-pepper eel along with a basket of crusty bread with which to soak up every last drop of sauce.
43 Rambla del Raval, 08001
+ 34 93 443 6579
suculent.com

⑧
The Green Spot, Barceloneta
Vibrant vegetarian

It's worth a trip to The Green Spot just to admire the minimalist, nature-inspired decor by Brazilian architect Isay Weinfeld. For vegetarians or vegans seeking meals that go beyond the basic salad, however, it could very well become a city favourite.

The approach to cooking here is geared towards flavour and texture, as well as making nutritious food that's deeply satisfying whether you're a vegetarian or not. Wood-fired pizza, tapas – with Mediterranean, Latin American and Asian influences – vibrant salads of wild greens and healthy pasta all lend themselves equally to a relaxed lunch or intimate dinner.
12 Carrer de la Reina Cristina, 08003
+ 34 93 802 5565
encompaniadelobos.com

⑩
Mano Rota, Poble-sec
Deftly prepared dining

Mano Rota (literally "broken hand") is a nod to a Spanish saying that means having a skill that comes easily. In the case of chef and owner Bernat Bermudo, it's not hard to determine the skill to which the restaurant's name refers.

After years of working under Michelin-starred chefs, Bermudo is equally at ease with Peruvian *aji* (green chilli sauce) and Thai curry as foie gras and truffles, making this high-end yet casual restaurant's menu a constant surprise and delight.
4 Carrer de la Creu dels Molers, 08004
+ 34 93 164 8041
manorota.com

⑪
Can Cisa/Bar Brutal, El Born
Small-plate smashes

In Spain, describing something as *brutal* (pronounced "brootal") is one of the highest forms of praise. So when your waiter asks you how your meal was, "brutal" is the perfect reply.

Can Cisa is the wine bar through which one enters Bar Brutal, where founders Max and Stefano Colombo – also of Xemei (*see page 26*) – serve small dishes from Spain and Italy. All the wines here are natural and many are also organic and biodynamic.

14 Carrer de la Princesa, 08003
+34 93 319 9881
cancisa.cat

⑫
El Chigre 1769, El Born
Cider house rules

While 1769 is the year in which the restaurant's building was constructed, *chigre* comes from the small sundry shops typical to mining towns of Asturias, where residents would gather to converse and drink cider.

Aptly, chef Fran Heras is Asturian and his partner Catalan, and this upscale tavern, complete with the sawdust-strewn floor of a cider bar, serves only products from these two distinct regions. The house speciality is fish, presented whole for approval before being served *a la plancha* (grilled).

7 Carrer dels Sombrerers, 08003
+34 93 782 6330
elchigre1769.com

Go on, just one more slice...

⑬
Bar Gresca, L'Antiga Esquerra
de l'Eixample
Catalan comfort food

The wine list at this informal
bistro boasts 400 new bottles
a month, something owner
and head chef Rafa Penya,
his tongue firmly in cheek,
attributes to him being "on
the right side of an alcoholic".
This sister space to the popular
Restaurante Gresca next door
serves Catalan fare, including a
sexed-up *bikini* (Spain's answer
to the toastie) dripping with
top-quality comté and *lomo
ibérico* (pork loin) from fêted
producer Manuel Maldonado.
  Our tip? Bag one of the
six stools overlooking the
spacious kitchen then soak up
the energy from the clatter of
dishes and the comfortingly
choreographed hubbub within.
230 Carrer de Provença, 08036
+34 93 451 6193

⑭
Bistrot Levante, Barri Gòtic
Laidback food and surrounds

Levante, named after the wind
that wafts from the eastern
Mediterranean, is a breath of
fresh air in a city brimming
with too-trendy tapas bars.
Dishes here are light, simple
and vegetable-laden with
plenty of za'atar, plus piles of
pitas and hummus served with
kumquat. The bean scene is top
notch too, with organic coffee
from a gleaming Milan-made
Rocket Espresso machine.
  Owner Emiliano Armani's
(*pictured*) training as both
architect and chef ensures
an easy equilibrium between
dishes and decor. The small
dining area is so light (and
filled with fig trees) that you
will be forgiven for thinking
you've strayed into the
charming square outside.
Placeta de Manuel Ribé, 08002
+34 93 858 2679
bistrotlevante.com

Seasons greetings
—
Menus in Catalonia change
with the seasons, as prized
ingredients come and go.
Grilled calçots (leek-like
onions), artichokes and peas
are typical in spring; tomatoes
and sardines in summer; wild
mushrooms in autumn; and sea
urchins in winter.

(16)

Gallito, Barceloneta
A shore thing

The open-air, vine-shaded terrace of Gallito offers sweeping views of Barceloneta, the city's most popular beach. Tucked below the W Barcelona Hotel and just steps from the sand, this sophisticated yet relaxed restaurant serves uncomplicated Spanish, Asian and Latin American flavours – a melange of dishes that's just as suited to a light summer lunch as a hearty supper.

Rustic design courtesy of the En Compañía de Lobos restaurant group – which also lays claim to The Green Spot (*see page 30*) – makes this restaurant a pleasure for both the eyes and the tastebuds.
19-21 Passeig del Mare Nostrum, 08039
+ 34 93 312 3585
encompaniadelobos.com/gallito

(15)

Estimar, El Born
Seafood paradise

At Estimar, Michelin-trained chef Rafa Zafra has made a temple to Neptune – a must for anyone wanting to dive into Catalonia's seafood. Each day the freshest catch possible is laid on ice on the countertop of the open kitchen, a showcase from which diners pick and craft their meals. Most seafood is sold by weight and rarer items such as *angulas* (baby eels), *percebes* (gooseneck barnacles) and *erizos de mar* (sea urchins) are available in season.
3 Carrer de Sant Antoni dels Sombrerers, 08003
+ 34 93 268 9197
restaurantestimar.com

Must-try
Fried anchovies at La Plata, Barri Gòtic
One of the city's longest-running tapas bars – it dates back to 1945 – draws crowds for its star dish (and one of only four things on the menu): *pescadito frito*. Anchovies fresh from Barcelona's docks are floured, fried whole and served piping hot. Best paired with a glass of house white.
barlaplata.com

Did someone say 'seconds'?

17

La Dama, L'Antiga Esquerra
de l'Eixample
Savour the sophistication

One would be hard-pressed
to find a more enchanting
restaurant in Barcelona than this
one, housed in the grandiose
modernista mansion Casa
Sayrach in the heart of the city.
A meal at La Dama is akin to
dining in the living room of
Barcelona's fin de siècle elite.

Spanish and Mediterranean
influences abound but, as
La Dama's chef hails from
Paris, the feeling here is
decidedly French. Sit on plush
banquettes surrounded by
soft candlelight and savour a
sophisticated dinner that could
last for hours if you allow it. We
recommend the roast pigeon
with an aged Spanish red.
*423-425 Avinguda Diagonal,
08008*
+ 34 93 209 6328
la-dama.com

(18)
La Taverna del Clínic, L'Antiga Esquerra de l'Eixample
Seasonal specialities

What began more than 10 years ago as a neighbourhood bar – slot machine and all – has become one of the best fine-dining restaurants in the city. Chef Toni Simôes (*pictured*) and his brother, sommelier Manuel "Manu" Simôes, expanded the tiny bar in 2014, building a full professional kitchen with a gleaming Charvet French cooking suite at its heart.

Diners can choose from various tasting menus and à la carte, all full of seasonal Catalan ingredients prepared with finesse and bolstered by everything from black garlic and caviar to celery sorbet and fugu broth.
155 Carrer del Rosselló, 08036
+34 93 410 4221
latavernadelclinic.com

(19)
Cometa Pla, Barri Gòtic
Natural goodness

From the intimate dining room and delicate food of restaurant Pla to the home-style tapas of Bar del Pla, Jaume Pla's respected family of restaurants offers excellent variety. At Cometa Pla, the inventive concept is chic and casual, and has Italian chef Giuseppe Padula (*pictured*) at the helm.

While the menu celebrates seasonal fruit and vegetables, the highlight here is the use of meat and seafood in a way that complements Mother Nature's offerings. Braised veal cheeks are paired with mushrooms and saffron rice, while the onion tarte tatin is a delectably flaky affair of caramelised onions, salted burrata foam and Italian bottarga fish roe.
5 Carrer del Cometa, 08002
+34 646 197 845
cometapla.cat

Local seafood

01 **Bacallà:** Salt cod isn't as common today as it once was. One of the best Catalan preparations is the *esqueixada*, a salad of chilled, shredded morsels of bacallà with onion, peppers, olives and tomatoes. Try the excellent version at classic tavern Set de Born.
setbarcelona.es

02 **Fried squid:** It's important to know your fried squid: it's usually prepared *a la romana* (large rings in a thick batter) or *a la andaluza* (small rings and tentacles dusted in flour). The latter's lighter, crispy coating is widely preferred in Barcelona; Bodega La Puntual does it perfectly.
bodegalapuntual.com

03 **Grilled Palamós prawns:** The red jumbo prawns fished in the Costa Brava village of Palamós are a true delicacy; a quick pass over a searing-hot *plancha* (griddle) and a pinch of coarse salt is all that's needed. Carballeira has the vintage ambience of a traditional Galician *marisquería* (seafood restaurant) and its prawns are superb.
carballeira.com

04 **Roasted monkfish:** Monkfish may be ugly but a meaty tail of *rap* (as it's known in Catalan) on your plate is a thing of beauty. Often referred to as "poor man's lobster", monkfish is dense and unctuous and often braised or roasted. At Senyor Parellada, the classic roasted monkfish with garlic is a must during summer months.
senyorparellada.com

Lunch
Midday meals

①

Fan Shoronpo, Gràcia
Plump for dumplings

In a sea of tapas, a lunch of *shoronpo* (soup dumplings) and ramen can be a welcome change of pace. Here the dumplings are hand-shaped to order and can be stuffed with the likes of pork, seafood, *jamón* and truffles, bursting with pork broth at first bite.

Start with a mix of *shoronpo* then move on to the other house speciality: *tantanmen* is a sesame and chilli-spiked ramen, laden with springy noodles and draped with tender sheets of braised *chashu* (pork belly).
28 Carrer de Sèneca, 08006
+34 93 009 2235
fanshoronpo.com

②

Entrepanes Díaz, Dreta de l'Eixample
Well-stuffed sandwiches

Barcelona's sandwiches are often simple, one-ingredient affairs – so when Entrepanes Díaz opened in 2015, people took notice. The vintage bar serves gourmet sandwiches filled with braised oxtail, pickled mussels, calamari and more.

The standout is the Antxón. A sandwich of *chistorra* (Basque-style cured sausage), it's topped with a poached egg and crispy matchstick potatoes and named after infamous Spanish art director Antxón Gómez, who helped design the restaurant's interior.
189 Carrer de Pau Claris, 08037
+34 93 415 7582

Must-try
Bomba de la Barceloneta at La Cova Fumada, Barceloneta
This hefty fried croquette of mashed potato and ground beef and pork with garlicky aioli and hot sauce is said to have been conceived at the classic Cova Fumada tapas bar in the heart of Barceloneta. So where better to try one?
+34 93 221 4061

③
Cafè Godot, Gràcia
French foundations

One of Barcelona's few restaurants to have earned the right to be called a bistro, Cafè Godot offers an extensive menu that changes throughout the day. There's plenty of French fare, as well as classic brunch options and an international lunch and dinner menu that has something for all palates.

The plate of duck confit with tiny black beluga lentils, mustard and spinach is an excellent homage to classic bistro cooking, while the green Thai curry scallops are just plain delicious. Add to this a design-conscious interior and relaxed atmosphere and this spot in Gràcia is a winner.
19 Carrer de Sant Domènec, 08012
+34 93 368 2036
cafegodot.com

④
Casa Lolea, El Born
Tapas with a twist

Sangria had a bad reputation in Barcelona as a sugar-loaded drink for tourists; its saviour was Casa Lolea, an intimate tapas bar opened by Bruno Balbás, one of the four founders of artisanal sangria brand Lolea. Pair your plates with a classic red, with notes of cinnamon and orange, or a sparkling variant made with Brut Cava, elderflower and apple.

The fare at Casa Lolea has a strong local identity but plenty of outside influences. Dishes such as truffle orzo (served risotto-style) join Spanish staples such as marinated sardines to define this modern but accessible style of inventive tapas.
49 Carrer de Sant Pere Més Alt, 08003
+34 93 624 1016
casalolea.com

⑤
La Paradeta, El Born
All you can eat

Seafood sold by weight and served market-style makes for the perfect unpretentious meal. The only challenge when eating at La Paradeta is choosing from the myriad options available.

Regular visitors, however, move through the ordering process like a breeze: the secret is to order all the seafood you can handle and request it be either grilled or fried, then order your drink and pay for the lot. Be warned: there's almost always a queue during meal times. Make the most of the wait by taking in the show as staff weigh out monkfish tails, tiny clams and tuna fillets.
7 Carrer Comercial, 08003
+34 93 268 1939
laparadeta.com

Food streets

01 **Carrer de Blai, Poble-sec:** Locals fill this popular street every evening for the ample outdoor seating and affordable *pintxos* (toothpick-skewered Basque bar food). At bars such as Blai Tonight, *pintxos* of morcilla sausage, scrambled egg with mushrooms and other varieties tempt you to try "just one more".

02 **Carrer del Parlament, Sant Antoni:** Along this three-block stretch you can enjoy a *vermut* at Els Sortidors del Parlament, brunch or lunch at Tarranà, a modern meal at Agust, an Aperol spritz on the terrace of Bar Calders or a late-night meal and cabaret at El Mama y La Papa.

03 **Carrer de la Mercè, Barri Gòtic:** One of the original tapas streets in Barcelona. Plump for pungent Asturian cheeses and cider-braised chorizo at Tasca El Corral, Galician-style boiled octopus with potato and shellfish at Bar Celta Pulperia or traditional tapas and home-style Catalan dishes at Belmonte.

In the markets
—
There are dozens of fresh markets in Barcelona but the cream of the crop are La Boqueria, Santa Caterina and Llibertat. Wander through the incredible displays, enjoy a fuss-free lunch and take some of the flavours home with you.
mercatsbcn.com

Tapas
Small wonders

01 02

03 04

05 06 07

08

09

10 11

12

Good things, small packages

Although it's now rarely served free with drinks, tapas is still a vital ingredient of the city's food scene. These plates are designed to be shared and can either accompany post-work beers or serve as a full dinner.

01 — 02 Bodega 1900, Sant Antoni: Old-school fare from chef Albert Adrià and brother Ferran (of El Bulli fame). There's also a more avant garde offering from their restaurant Tickets, across the street.
bodega1900.com

03 — 04 Jai-Ca, Barceloneta: A no-frills spot near the beach for ice-cold beer, fried baby squid, grilled clams and dozens of other classic tapas.
barjaica.com

05 — 07 Bar Bodega Quimet, Gràcia: An intimate bar with wine from the barrel and a variety of excellent hot and cold tapas.
+34 93 218 4189

08 Bar del Pla, El Born: Authentic tapas such as squid-ink croquettes, chicken-stuffed *canelón* pasta or fried eggs with Catalan sausages.
bardelpla.cat

09 — 11 El Vaso de Oro, Barceloneta: Waiters in epaulets serve traditional tapas and local lager. One of the few classic *cervecerías* (beer-focused bars) remaining in Barceloneta.
vasodeoro.com

12 Quimet y Quimet, Poble-sec: This tiny bar specialises in preserved foods. Think marinated quail and foie gras with black volcanic salt.
+34 93 442 3142

Coffee shops
Daily grind

1

Caravelle, El Raval
Brewing coffee and beer

Australian-born Zim Sutton and Poppy Da Costa parked their caravan in Barcelona and opened a more permanent restaurant-turned-café and microbrewery in 2012. Care and thought are evident in every inch of the space, from the homemade cold brew to the milk, delivered daily from the nearby village of L'Ametlla del Vallès. Don't miss the Moroccan-style baked eggs and drop by in the evening for a tipple; the Midnight Run IPA is a showstopper.
31 Carrer del Pintor
Fortuny, 08001
+34 93 317 9892
caravelle.es

②

Espai Joliu, Poblenou
Back to basics

In step with the industrial character of Poblenou, this plant-filled café is all stripped-back walls, rustic chairs and plentiful pottery and prints. Despite the bohemian feel it's not style over substance: owner Lucía López makes a mean coffee with beans from nearby roaster Nømad (*see page 43*).

After polishing off a cinnamon roll and macchiato out the back, take a moment to sift through the thoughtful selection of independent magazines or browse the myriad cacti, succulents and tropical plants for sale.
95 Carrer de Badajoz, 08005
+34 93 023 2492

③

Satan's Coffee Corner, Barri Gòtic
Hellishly good

"So many speciality cafés have such a soft edge to them," says the owner of Satan's, Marcos Bartolomé, with a chuckle. "My brand of cheeky fun is a way of putting them on edge instead." The sign advising "no wi-fi, no decaf and no bullshit" is more honest manifesto than hostile welcome; here the tone is nonchalant but never in a too-cool-to-serve-you way.

One of the pioneers of Barcelona's coffee cadre, Bartolomé ensures his beans, pastries and Japanese breakfast are all top notch. While satellite versions of his café pop up in other spaces around the city, this is his permanent home.
11 Carrer de l'Arc de Sant Ramon del Call, 08002
satanscoffee.com

④

Federal Café, Barri Gòtic
Down Under coffee culture

The success of the first Federal Café in Sant Antoni awakened the city's once-sleepy breakfast scene back in 2010. This Barri Gòtic branch, however, is more of a favourite for residents than the international brunch crowd.

Aussie couple Tommy Tang and Crick King christened their café after Federal, a beautiful town near Byron Bay, and the menu has a typically antipodean mix of Italian, Asian and Middle Eastern flavours. Decorating and designing the furniture themselves, the duo have also imported another Australian custom: the open-all-day kitchen. No flat white feels complete without a freshly baked lamington cake.
11 Passatge de la Pau, 08002
+ 34 93 280 8171
federalcafe.es

*I do love
Federal Café's
flat whites*

⑤

Nømad Coffee, El Born
Unassuming excellence

A reputation as Spain's most decorated barista prompted Jordi Mestre to open this coffee-tasting post in 2014. He's since expanded with a second café and roaster in Poblenou and another outpost in El Raval – but this first, low-key location remains simple and on the right side of ceremonious.

Small wicker stools line the bar, where coffee is served on square green-marble slabs. Two quirks to note: there's no sugar in sight (at Nømad it's nothing short of sacrilege) and the lane on which the café is located is locked in the evenings and on weekends, limiting visits to weekdays before 17.30. If you're dying for a Nømad kick, however, don't forget its other outposts.
12 Passatge Sert, 08003
nomadcoffee.es

Food shopping

01 Vila Viniteca 'La Teca', El Born: With more than 300 cheeses from across Spain and beyond – and a cornucopia of other artisanal food products, from Iberian *jamón* and organic olive oil to canned razor clams and Ibiza sea salt – La Teca is a gourmet paradise. After shopping, take a seat at the tasting bar (better yet, ask for a spot in the 15th-century wine cellar) for a unique cheese-and-wine pairing.
vilaviniteca.es

02 La Campana, El Born: An enchanting old-fashioned sweet shop on Carrer de la Princesa that has been grinding almonds into *torró* (nougat) since 1890. Go authentic with the hard Alicante variant of whipped egg whites and whole almonds, or the rich and creamy Jijona style made with almond paste. Around the festive season it makes a great gift – just don't forget to bring some home for yourself.
lacampanadesde1890.com

03 Casa Gispert, El Born: Step back in time via the ornate façade of this ancient and inviting dry-goods shop in the heart of El Born. Casa Gispert is recognised as one of the best artisanal food shops in Europe and still roasts nuts daily in the original wood-fired oven from 1851. The roasted almonds are the star product but the rich coffee, chocolate-dipped confit fruit and aromatic spice display are equally alluring.
casagispert.com

①
Pastisseria Hofmann, El Born
Flaky favourites

This small shop should be a mandatory stop for any pastry lover. Authentic farmhouse butter and true culinary prowess make the treats among the city's best.

Classic croissants also come with various stuffings: mascarpone cheese, raspberry jam, dulce de leche or chocolate burst out of the chewy centre and a crust so perfectly flaky that you'll need several napkins. Best enjoyed while people-watching along the Passeig del Born.
44 Carrer dels Flassaders, 08003
+34 93 268 8221
hofmann-bcn.com

②
Granja Dulcinea, Barri Gòtic
Chocolate and churros

It's a little-known fact that the world's first chocolate factory was in Barcelona. Cacao arrived in Spain in the 1500s, aboard ships returning from Columbus's expedition to the New World, and in 1777 a workshop for roasting and grinding chocolate was built outside the city.

Barcelona's love affair with chocolate has endured for centuries and traditional cafés specialising in golden fried churros – dusted with sugar and served with thick, bittersweet hot chocolate – boomed in the 20th century. Granja Dulcinea opened in 1941 and the vibe has changed little since, with dark-wood trim and bow-tied, white-shirted staff.
2 Carrer de Petritxol, 08002
+34 93 302 6824
granjadulcinea.com

③
Baluard Praktik, Dreta de l'Eixample
Sourdough source

The name Baluard has long been synonymous with excellent, organic, slow-fermented sourdough bread, something that until recently was a rare find in Barcelona. Following in the footsteps of three generations of bakers, Anna Bellsolà opened the first Baluard bakery on Carrer del Baluard in 2007, then in 2014 she fired up the ovens at her new outpost inside the Hotel Praktik near Passeig de Gràcia (for which Baluard provides all the baked goods). Grab a *bocadillo de jamón* (ham sandwich) or a dose of something sweet and enjoy it in the hotel's elegant garden.
279 Carrer de Provença, 08037
+34 93 488 0061
hotelpraktikbakery.com

❶

Mont Bar, L'Antiga Esquerra de l'Eixample
Epic wine list

This modern bistro boasts a list of more than 300 wines from myriad international regions. The vast offering provides endless pairing opportunities with chef Domenico Ungaro's modern menu of tapas and larger plates.

Served in a warmly lit space at either the smooth marble bar, the large communal table or an intimate pavement terrace table for two, the colourful and creative dishes have become chef Ungaro's signature. Try the smoked sardines with squid-ink tuile, mango and yoghurt or the savoury *mochi* of rich sobrasada sausage with walnuts and Mahón cheese.
220 Carrer de la Diputació, 08011
+34 93 323 9590
montbar.com

②

Mitja Vida, Sarrià-Sant Gervasi
Stay a while

A narrow and bustling neighbourhood bar, Mitja Vida ("half life" in Catalan) is pure Barcelona. Named after the substantial portion of one's life that should be merrily spent at its long bar, this popular spot opened as a follow-up to the original and miniscule Morro Fi *vermuteria* in Eixample.

Mitja Vida serves Morro Fi-brand artisan *vermut* and *conservas* – tinned savouries that are typically paired with the tipple. Peel open a can of razor clams, baby squid or mussels packed in vinegary *escabetx* marinade and taste one of the most classic flavour combinations in the canon of Barcelonan cuisine.
62 Carrer de Brusi, 08006
morrofi.cat

④

Balius, Poblenou
Gastro cocktails

This cocktail and *vermut* bar is located in a former pharmacy of the same name. Balius is decked out in *modernisme*-era tiles and retro banquettes that give this self-proclaimed "gastro cocktail bar" both class and kitsch.

A variety of *vermut* supplements a list of craft cocktails, from the classic rye martini to a twist on the mint julep that replaces bourbon with Cynar, grapefruit, lime and bitters. The food offering is minimal but eclectic, with a tapas of miso-infused meatballs with mushroom mousse, and a dish of salt-cod brandade with quail egg.
196 Carrer de Pujades, 08005
+34 93 315 8650
baliusbar.com

③

Cervecería Jazz, Poble-sec
Crafty drinks

Long before Poble-sec began filling with modern restaurants and charming dive bars, Cervecería Jazz was serving craft beer – think Belgian blondes and British bitters – to anyone keen to trade the busy Avinguda del Paral.lel for the quiet Carrer de Margarit beneath Montjuïc.

Exposed brick, brass and wood under soft lamplight make this enticing bar ideal for a relaxed night with friends. The list of beers is by no means limited to classics: there's an ever-changing range of brews on tap, from IPAS to imperial stouts, which arrive at this little bar from all across the globe.
43 Carrer de Margarit, 08004
+34 93 443 3259
cerveceriajazz.com

Roll up, roll up

Every first weekend of the month, designers, musicians, food trucks and fashion brands pop up at the Palo Alto Market. This old factory in Poblenou is the place for "Made in Barcelona" clothing and art, as well as top-notch street food.
paloaltomarket.com

Ⓢ
Paradiso, El Born
Clandestine cocktails

Paradiso is hidden behind the heavy wooden door of an old-school pastrami bar's antique refrigerator. The speakeasy is one of the most highly regarded cocktail bars in Barcelona, with award-winning bartender Giacomo Giannotti (*pictured*) at the helm of the elegant haunt.

Clouds of dry-ice smoke waft over delicate and eccentric serving vessels – from Japanese teapots to crystal skulls – and a breadth of cocktails such as the Salvador Dalí Manhattan (a sweet-and-bitter take on the classic) and the Breakfast in Kentucky (made from egg white, bacon, bourbon and maple syrup, it's far better than it sounds). If you get peckish ask for a sourdough sandwich, made with pastrami from the up-front deli, which is run by Eixample-based restaurant Rooftop Smokehouse.

4 Carrer de Rera Palau, 08003
+34 93 360 7222
paradiso.cat

Did someone say pastrami?

Retail
—— Spending time

Stray from Barcelona's well-trodden retail trails and you'll find a parallel universe of artisans, ambitious young brands and age-old merchants. The best small-scale shops and studios often sit conveniently close to main streets and Barcelona's spirit of solidarity has led to like-minded retailers clustering in specific districts. Eixample overflows with upscale fashion, El Born is a bastion of up-and-comers, Poblenou houses modern and vintage design, and Barri Gòtic has long been an old-guard stronghold.

Apart from the geographical spread you should also factor the city's archaic opening hours into your shopping schedule. With late-morning starts, the shutters coming down for two or three-hour lunchbreaks and a stubborn ban on Sunday trading, the fitful daily pace is a frustration to the city's desire to be a modern capital. Your best bet is to concentrate on one particular district and shop only in the morning or late afternoon. Save the middle of the day for what Spaniards do best: a leisurely lunch timed to end as the shops reopen for the evening shift.

Menswear
Wardrobe essentials

❶
Norman Vilalta, L'Antiga Esquerra de l'Eixample
Footwear with flair

From humble beginnings in the Patagonian port of Puerto Madryn, Norman Vilalta (*pictured*) has become Barcelona's most progressive shoemaker. The Argentinian learned his craft in Florence and channels his natural artistic flair into a bespoke approach to classics such as the Chelsea boot, Derby and Oxford.

"Using old tools and modern technology allows me to invent something new," says Vilalta. He embraces rubber soles, patterned materials and the amalgamation of artisanal techniques, believing that tradition should be a guide but never a constraint to his craft.
5 Carrer d'Enric Granados, 08007
+34 93 323 4014
normanvilalta.com

② The Outpost, Dreta de
l'Eixample
Impeccable selection

Following a 22-year career
inside the gruelling Milan
fashion machine, Pep Esteva
(*pictured*) decided to move
back to his home city for
a long-overdue change. "I
wanted to do something that
no one else was doing," he says,
a hint of rebellion in his voice.
That something turned out to
be a well-designed men's shoes
and accessories shop, which
opened in 2008 and now stocks
brands from Ateliers Heschung
and Moscot to Issey Miyake.

The fit-out from interior
designer Pilar Líbano
combines classic elements
with contemporary flourishes
and is impeccably filled with
everything from the finest
shoes, leather goods, hats, bags,
ties and sunglasses through
to swimwear and bathrobes.
Then there's Pep himself –
his fashion knowledge fits the
shop like a well-tailored glove
so don't be shy about asking
him for advice.
*281 bis, Carrer del
Rosselló, 08037
+34 93 457 7137
theoutpostbcn.com*

③
Wer-Haus, Dreta de l'Eixample
More than just fashion

Thumbing its nose at
the conventional idea of
extravagance, Wer-Haus sits
teasingly close to the haughty
high street of Passeig de
Gràcia. Frenchmen Nicolas
Rossi (*pictured*) and Jean-
Antoine Palagos joined forces
with Catalan film-maker
Marc Miró to carve out
their fashionable new niche
in a former garage, which
now encompasses a gallery,
bookshop, small restaurant
and elevated fashion area.

The brands at Wer-Haus
include Lemaire, Raf Simons,
Études Studio and Adidas,
while the printed matter lining
the shelves in the bookshop
focuses on fashion and
photography. Time your visit
to coincide with your midday
macchiato – the talented on-site
barista and tasty lunch menu
draw in plenty of foot traffic.
*287 Carrer d'Aragó, 08009
+34 93 515 0298
wer-haus.com*

Mixed
Something for everyone

①
Loewe, Dreta de l'Eixample
Luxurious leathers

Loewe started life as a collective of leather artisans from Madrid but has since claimed its rightful place on Barcelona's commercial landscape as Spain's flag-bearer for luxury retail goods. It's worth a trip just to see the playful *modernista* façade of the Lluís Domènech i Montaner-designed building.

Invigorated by the boundless vision of creative director Jonathan Anderson, the men's and women's leather collections are of singular craftsmanship and have plenty of colour and chutzpah. The label's ongoing love affair with this city is immortalised in its ever-sleek Barcelona bag, released in 2015.

35 Passeig de Gràcia, 08008
+34 93 216 0400
loewe.com

②

Santa Eulalia, Dreta de
l'Eixample
Proud tradition

This heritage luxury fashion
house is one of the few
original icons left on the city's
increasingly international scene.
Boasting four generations of
retail acumen, the multibrand
department store has been in
this exquisite space since 1944
(the original shop opened just
off La Rambla in 1843).

An in-house tailor nods
to tradition while Balenciaga,
Moncler, Kenzo, Acne
Studios and Tom Ford are
just a sample of the labels on
offer. Meanwhile a bistro and
champagne bar offer a discreet
oasis upstairs. "We ensure
that everyone is made to feel
comfortable," says owner and
director Luis Sans.
93 Passeig de Gràcia, 08008
+34 93 215 0674
santaeulalia.com

④

Darial, Dreta de l'Eixample
Rich pickings

A shop, gallery and restaurant
rolled into one, Darial is also
where you'll spot some of
the city's most well-heeled
residents. It oozes opulence and
savoir-faire, not least through
its modish and entrepreneurial
Georgian owners.

Listing all the laudable
labels under its roof would
take all day but we admire the
latest threads by Sacai, Oliver
Spencer and Yohji Yamamoto,
the Spanish womenswear
designs of Delpozo and the
glittering array of jewellery.
The bedazzling outfits are
matched by the futuristic
fit-out, which was created in
collaboration with designer
Djaba Diassamidze.
37 Carrer d'Ausiàs Marc, 08010
+ 34 663 833 767
darial.com

③

Shon Mott, Dreta de
l'Eixample
A family affair

Brothers Kiko and Pep Buxó
Genero (*pictured, Pep on left*)
combine their family's textile
heritage with backgrounds in
fashion and industrial design.
Their men's and womenswear
collections are both marked by
functional forms, neutral tones
and Mediterranean charm.

Each garment is made in
Spain and Kiko extolls the
advantage of being a small
family firm. "We treat our
customers with familiarity; we
want people to feel as if they're
dropping in to see a friend."
157 Carrer de Pau Claris, 08037
+ 34 93 461 8232
shonmott.com

⑤

La Comercial, El Born
Collective effort

Comprising six shopfronts in
El Born, La Comercial flaunts
the diversity and dimensions
of a fashion empire. But while
it seems to have taken over the
whole block, founder Carlos del
Barrio ensures that his colony
of shops has an independent
air, with separate spaces for
men, women, accessories and
homeware.

Del Barrio pioneered high-
end retail in the *barri* and still
stacks his racks with big names:
Balmain and Kenzo for men;
Missoni, Vivienne Westwood
and Alexander McQueen for
women. Take time to peruse the
impressive array of perfumes
and accessories too.
52 and 73 Carrer del Rec, 08003
(women's and menswear)
4 Carrer del Bonaire, 08003
(homeware)
+ 34 93 268 3367
lacomercial.info

Womenswear
Fashion favourites

①

Cortana, Dreta de l'Eixample
Fairytale pieces

A whimsical ode to the age-old textile industry of the Balearic Islands, Cortana stocks pieces imbued with founder and designer Rosa Esteva's Mallorcan provenance. Her label combines waif-like silhouettes with a sense of pared-back wonder and the design of her subterranean shop, just a stone's throw from Passeig de Gràcia, augments the sense of awe.

Designed by her father and brother's architectural studio Esteva i Esteva, the shop stands out for the way clothes are hung on metallic poles that descend from the ceiling, showing off Esteva's affinity with silk, wool and cashmere. Her fairytale vision also extends to a successful range of bridalwear, while patterns are inspired by the designer's watercolour paintings.
290 Carrer de Provença, 08008
+ 34 93 487 2070
cortana.es

②

Coquette, El Born
French-inspired elegance

"I was born and raised in San Sebastián, a city known for its sober elegance," says Coquette's founder, Isabel Campelo. That elegance permeates her boutique, with clothing from APC, Isabel Marant Étoile and Masscob reflecting her French-inspired vision of femininity.

Campelo strives to provide a personal touch to all three of her shops: the second sits on nearby Carrer del Bonaire, the third in Sarrià-Sant Gervasi. All enjoy a loyal, sophisticated clientele.
65 Carrer del Rec, 08003
+ 34 93 319 2976
coquettebcn.com

③
About Arianne, Bogatell
Fancy footwork

Ariadna Guirado and Ernest Vidal keep their studio door open to anyone interested in artisan shoes. The workshop and retail space is their way of ensuring that customers receive closer attention than they would on a busy shopping strip. "We're all about the finer details and we love getting to know the people who wear our shoes," says Guirado.

Manufactured in Spain's footwear heartland of Elche, near Alicante, the designs blend traditional sensibilities with the more modern pursuit of supreme comfort, and are especially popular in North America, Japan and Australia. There's even a vegan range in cotton and organic resin.
84 Carrer de Pallars, 08018
+34 692 784 092
aboutarianne.com

La Tercera
—
A small pocket of El Born hosts a cluster of independently minded shops brimming with pieces by Barcelona's up-and-coming designers. One of the best is La Tercera's showroom, with its leather handbags by Name: and Lubochka. Wander the cramped blocks to discover plenty more.

④
Sita Murt, Dreta de l'Eixample
Tight knits

Turning her family's textile-manufacturing dynasty into a chic designer label, Sita Murt quickly became one of Catalonia's most savvy (and successful) prêt-à-porter players. The late designer is renowned for her magic with wool and mohair knits and left a formidable fashion legacy: her collections are sold in some of the world's best department stores, from Moscow and Melbourne to Paris and Tokyo.

There are three other outposts in Barcelona (in El Born and Sarrià-Sant Gervasi) but this one in Eixample is by far the best. Some of her clothes were featured in Woody Allen's film *Vicky Cristina Barcelona*.
242 Carrer de Mallorca, 08008
+34 93 215 2231
sitamurt.com

⑤
Lydia Delgado, Gràcia
Designed to a tee

A former opera-house dancer, Lydia Delgado has always lived at her own tempo. When she launched a bright and buoyant range of T-shirts it was simply another form of fun-filled expression, turning into a fully fledged atelier in 1987.

Her range uses a unique brand of ebullient colours (she dyes many of her Italian-sourced fabrics herself) and frequent doses of fine silk embroidery. "I don't like to emulate other brands," says the designer. "I prefer to live in my own world, which is as much of a luxury in fashion as it is in real life." Look out for her art lining the walls and the equally bright clothing collaboration with her daughter Miranda Makaroff.
28 Carrer de Sèneca, 08006
+34 93 218 1630
lydiadelgado.es

Concept
What's the big idea?

(1)
Alfons & Damián,
Sarrià-Sant Gervasi
Internal workings

Interior designers Alfons Tost
and Damián Sánchez serviced
an esteemed private clientele
before opening a design shop,
in-house florist and decorating
studio in 2015. "We wanted to
share unique pieces that were
practically impossible to find
anywhere else in Barcelona,"
says Tost.

Just a short distance from
Avinguda Diagonal, the shop's
sumptuousness extends across
every inch of its interior with
perfectly restored antiques,
Karim Rashid-designed
ornaments and playful glassware
by Artel. The space has quickly
become the emporium of choice
for the affluent folks who call
Sarrià-Sant Gervasi home.
7 Passatge de Marimon, 08021
+34 93 414 2619
alfonsdamian.com

② **Nuovum, El Raval**
Design showcase

This enchanting emporium both looks and feels like a hive of modern Spanish design: the walls feature hexagonal wooden shelving filled with the creations of the country's up-and-coming designers. José Miguel Sevilla (*pictured*) has built what he calls a "network of busy bees", from Madrid and Valencia to San Sebastián.

"We provide an antidote to the surfeit of tawdry souvenir shops," he says showing off the hand-crafted bags, jewellery and ornaments. "There are lots of independent retailers moving into El Raval. The nearby galleries and cultural institutions make the district a natural destination for design."
30 Carrer del Pintor
Fortuny, 08001
+34 93 412 6411
nuovum.com

③ **Mica, El Born**
Small pleasures

Most of the finely made products displayed inside this narrow shop are pint-sized, making it the ideal place to pick up souvenirs that will fit into your carry-on. Graphic designer Judit Reig opened the petite repository in 2017, filling it with Falcon enamelware, Siwa paper accessories, Serax ceramics and children's toys and books, as well as a gold-standard array of notebooks and stationery. Her partner, a blacksmith, designed the lighting and shelving.
47 Carrer de Trafalgar, 08010
+34 93 119 3426
mica.barcelona

④ **Jaime Beriestain, Dreta de l'Eixample**
Themed treasures

After years of decorating homes and hotels, Barcelona's most dapper Chilean opened his own concept store. A well-appointed temple to his fine taste, it includes a buzzing restaurant and secluded cocktail bar at the back.

The area is loosely divided into conceptual spaces that include the sea, countryside, and mountains, offering a plethora of designer items procured during Beriestain's travels. His eponymous brand is certainly diverse, with porcelain dinnerware, lighting, scented candles, soap and linen, as well as chocolate, nougat and other pantry goodies to further sweeten the range.
167 Carrer de Pau Claris, 08037
+34 93 515 0782
beriestain.com

①

Casa Atlântica, Gràcia
Ceramics and more

A blurring of the design vernacular along the Portuguese and Galician border, Casa Atlântica pays homage to the "common artisanship" that has kept the ceramic urns firing in that region for centuries.

From a workshop downstairs, founders Lester Barreto, Belén Martínez and Pedro Dias produce multi-hued crockery and plant pots, stocked alongside lampshades, mirrors, rugs and baskets, all hailing from their homeland. The flock of wall-mounted black *andorinhas* (swallows) is a further nod to tradition, while their opening times (12.00 to 20.00) are a modern rarity in this lunch-break-loving city.
7 Carrer de la Llibertat, 08012
+ 34 93 667 7977
casaatlantica.es

⑤
Clay Concept Store, El Born
Global selection

Glassware from Syria, chairs from Morocco, Andalucían ceramics and linen towels and cushions from Antalya in Turkey: Clay's shelves are a cross-section of the world's most time-honoured artisans.

Sat on a street that has been transformed by a community of like-minded concept stores, this former urban stable retains its rustic veneer. The three owners (from Madrid, Cádiz and Colombia) keep the interior cosy and comfortable with woven seagrass mats, snug Peruvian alpaca jumpers and clothing by YMC and Ganni.
11 Carrer dels Banys Vells, 08003
+ 34 93 164 8782

②
Noak Room, Poblenou
Fully furnished

Swede Martin Noaksson and his Madrileña wife Sara Salas (*pictured*) opened their Scandi-flavoured vintage furniture shop in a former carpenter's workshop in Poblenou, attracted by the *barri*'s post-industrial charm (*see page 70*). They make regular trips to Norway, Denmark and Sweden to keep the lofty space filled with cabinets, tables, sofas and bric-a-brac.

Across the road their second space, Industry, feels closer to home. "We have an intense artistic community," says Salas. "Industry provides a platform for the neighbourhood's makers, who represent more than a dozen different nationalities."
69 Carrer de Roc Boronat, 08005
+ 34 93 309 5300
noakroom.com

③
Kettal, Dreta de l'Eixample
Outdoor settings

This much-loved Spanish outdoor furniture brand can be found in gardens and by hotel pools around the globe. Its flagship showroom boasts its best collaborations, from Patricia Urquiola to Jasper Morrison, all the while underlining its commitment to local production.

The family-run firm barely resembles the no-frills, austere brand that first appeared on Spanish beaches in the 1960s. Created by enterprising Catalan businessman Manuel Alorda, Kettal is now in the hands of his son Alex, who has placed sleek designs and product customisation at the forefront of the company's ethos. Design cues are taken from around the world, resulting in pieces that are suited to sunny outdoor settings from the Mediterranean to the Maldives.
316 Carrer d'Aragó, 08009
+ 34 93 488 1080
kettal.com

Paving the way
—
Admiring the Gaudí-designed *panots* (paving stones) in Passeig de Gràcia? Step into renowned homeware shop Cubiñá, which stocks a ceramic selection echoing the hallowed street pavers. The old printing press also carries furniture, lighting and shelving.
cubinya.es

④
AOO, Gràcia
Reworking the classics

A passion for procuring the finest handmade crafts from Spain and abroad inspired designers Marc Morro (*pictured*) and Oriol Villar to open AOO in 2013. The duo decided to pare back the offering several years later, eschewing an earlier shop concept that paid homage to other first-class native designers; the spotlight is now focused on their own pieces.

Reinterpreting age-old designs, their studio is best known for its Pepitu deckchair, the Salvador cane chair (perfect for porches) and an array of sturdy stools. Their creations offer a contemporary touch and are as vested with functionality as aesthetic appeal.

8 Carrer de Sèneca, 08006
+34 93 250 8254
aoobarcelona.com

BD Barcelona Design, Poblenou
Catalan design mecca

Not many places can claim to stock original designs by Gaudí and Dalí but then this shop, showroom and studio has always been different. It was opened in the 1970s by a group of architects, who created an avant garde parade of lighting and furniture that was snapped up by Spain's burgeoning post-Franco bourgeoisie.

Ten years later the firm reproduced some of Gaudí's Calvet and Batlló furniture designs, adding Dalí's beyond-quirky creations (check out the lamb-shaped bedside table) several years later. More modern collaborations include pieces by Jaime Hayon and Doshi Levien.

126 Carrer de Ramon Turró, 08005
+34 93 458 6909
bdbarcelona.com

⑥

It Reminds Me of Something, Barri Gòtic
Creative showcase

That something you're reminded of here could be a high-end contemporary-art gallery but don't be fooled: this is definitely a shop. Rubén López (*pictured*) opened this space to celebrate the artistic endeavours of craftsmen in Barcelona and beyond.

"Every imaginative item has its own tale," says López, who happily narrates the back-stories of sculptures designed by Damián Quiroga or the sinuous wood-carved furniture pieces by Brucc. The only pre-requisite for being showcased here is that each artisan must both design and produce their piece, making it an axis of unfettered creativity energy.
9 Carrer dels Sagristans, 08002
+34 93 318 6020
itremindsmeofsomething.com

⑦

Brutus de Gaper, Bogatell
Vast design collection

Dutchmen Niels Jansen (*pictured*) ditched his career in the technology sector in 2016 to delve into a lifelong passion for design. "This is where our heart is," says Jansen, who, together with co-founder Ron Van Melick, spent two years accumulating stock in order to fill the huge warehouse (be sure to request a visit to the equally vast second hall next door).

Lightshades hang from the roof like a psychedelic canopy, while the floor overflows with Dutch designers such as Cees Braakman, as well as Nordic and Italian pieces that reflect their love of retro rationalism. A restorer works diligently out back and a selection of exotic plants mirrors the pair's wish to keep growing.
60 Carrer de Pamplona, 08005
+34 93 639 3013
brutusdegaper.com

① **Iriarte Iriarte, El Born**
Handmade bags

The owner of this leather-bag shop, Carolina López Gordillo Iriarte (*pictured*), creates each handbag, satchel and purse by hand, tanning the leather, slicing the shapes and stitching them all together. Each creation features recycled clasps and rivets and is the result of an all-natural production process.

The made-to-order approach means you may wait up to five weeks to receive your bag – but it's worth the wait.
12 Carrer dels Cotoners, 08002
+34 93 319 8175
iriarteiriarte.com

⑧
Marset, Sarrià-Sant Gervasi
Let there be lights

Tucked away behind the ritzy shopfronts lining affluent Carrer de Santaló, this showroom is flooded with bright ideas. It wasn't until the 1970s that Paco Marset produced his first lamps by using his family's manufacturing business as a foundation but he soon transformed the firm into an award-winning pantheon of iconic design.

Marset's mushroom-shaped FollowMe lamp seems to be mandatory in most Catalan households but we also love the innovative design of the swivelling Theia lamp and the striking silhouettes of the Pleat Box hanging lampshades. The latter were designed by ceramic studio Apparatu and cast different hues of light according to the enamel painted on their interior.
56 Carrer de Santaló, 08021
+34 93 200 5726
marset.com

② **La Manual Alpargatera, Barri Gòtic**
Timeless espadrilles

Visiting Spain without snapping up a pair of espadrilles could be considered a form of souvenir sacrilege. Thankfully La Manual is happy to oblige with all colours, styles and sizes.

City folk once shunned espadrilles as the footwear of farmers but then this family-run business opened in 1941. Made from natural fibres – including hemp, jute and esparto grass – and then sealed with cotton and linen, the shoes transcend fashion trends. A similar sandal was found on 4,000-year-old human remains in a cave near Granada, while the Mossos d'Esquadra regional police force wear a blue pair with their dress uniform.
7 Carrer d'Avinyó, 08002
+34 93 301 0172
lamanualalpargatera.es

③
Siesta Arte y Objetos, El Raval
Promoting local artisans

Supporting small-scale craftsmanship, Argentinian émigré Mercedes Rodrigo provides a platform for some of the city's most skilled artisans. The illuminated cabinets of this former haberdashery abound with ceramics such as teapots, plates and sculptures, many made by Norwegian, Japanese and German expats who call Barcelona home. The jewellery is by students from the nearby Massana art and design school.

"People ask if this is a gallery or a shop," says Rodrigo. "It's both. Everything is for sale – except my dog." And don't be afraid to ask to see more: there's plenty of treasure stowed in the drawers and cupboards.

18 Carrer de Ferlandina, 08001
+34 93 317 8041
siestaweb.com

④
Sombrerería Obach, Barri Gòtic
Wholly headwear

This hatter's crammed window displays are juxtaposed by its austere interior, prompting many customers to wonder whether they've mistakenly stepped into a storeroom. The Obach family, who have been running the shop since 1924, are quick to settle any confusion, asking clients about their preferred style, taking measurements and then bringing out as many hats as you desire from behind the mirrored cabinets.

The headwear is all handmade in Seville and Alicante. One of the most popular models, El Clásico, was favoured by founder José Obach and is available in eight different colours.

2 Carrer del Call, 08002
+34 93 318 4094
sombreriaobach.es

⑤
Ganiveteria Roca, Barri Gòtic
Honing instinct

The marble threshold of this hardware specialist bears the words "*casa de confiança*" ("house of trust") and the shop attendants do nothing to contradict that welcome. The shop's expertise in sharpened blades dates back to 1911 and has led to an accumulation of more than 6,000 products to help you get a closer shave, cut your meat more finely or just have the sharpest tool in the shed.

Other small details, including the chairs reserved for waiting customers, are a reminder of a more considered customer-service model. But it's the sharp focus on product knowledge that has kept this shop at the cutting edge.

3 Plaça del Pi, 08002
+34 93 302 1241
ganiveteriaroca.com

Eternal flame
—
Amid Barcelona's sometimes fiery debate on gentrification, the flame of centuries-old candle shop Cereria Subirà burns ever bright. Dating back to 1761, the pastel-hued interior is steeped in scents from candles that are both practical and pretty.
+34 93 315 2606

⑥

Etnia Barcelona, El Born
Bask in the shades

A bona fide feast for the eyes, Etnia's seven-storey flagship combines a vivid palette, frames inspired by style icons and a strong family history of making eyewear. David Pellicer started his far-sighted brand intending to add a splash of colour to the predominantly dark offering of shades.

The brand is proud of its Barcelonan heritage but has a strong global presence too: it exports up to 90 per cent of its ever-expanding range, which includes capsule collections dedicated to cultural figures such as Nobuyoshi Araki and Jean-Michel Basquiat. If you're looking to snag a pair, ask to try them out on the rooftop terrace.
1-3 Carrer de l'Espaseria, 08003
+34 93 018 6614
etniabarcelona.com

Pots off the press
——
If you want to do more than grab some finished pottery, get your hands on the clay itself with a class at Atuell Ceramica. Located in Gràcia, it has turned out some of the city's best up-and-coming ceramicists.
atuell.com

⑦

Working in the Redwoods, El Born
Pots of distinction

For her smooth ceramics line, industrial designer Miriam Cernuda (*pictured*) draws inspiration from the earthy tones and textures of her childhood home on the Costa Brava. The white-walled workshop and retail space divides Cernuda's creations into two lines.

The Basic collection comprises pastel-painted kitchen accessories, homeware and lamps finished with both glossy and matt lead-free glazes. Her Weathered range features more telluric tones, using white clay and natural pigments to highlight the beauty of the Earth's core materials. Cernuda is often commissioned for specially made restoration pieces and stocks her space with a smattering of complementary items, including accessories and wooden utensils.
4 Carrer de Lluís el Piadós, 08003
+34 606 587 108
workingintheredwoods.com

⑧
Après Ski, El Born
Painted jewellery perfection

After a spell working for Alianto and Lydia Delgado's fashion label (*see page 54*), Lucía Vergara (*pictured*) launched her own brand of painted jewellery, sold in shops and galleries across the US, Japan and Australia. "Everyone working for me is trained in a variant of the Japanese lacquer technique, which means you'll usually find us painting jewellery at a table on the shop floor," says the designer.

Vergara's sources of inspiration include flora and fauna, as well as frequent visits to decorative-arts museums. Aside from her necklaces and bracelets made mainly from wood, vintage resin and brass, there's also a small assortment of painted ceramics.
11 Carrer dels Vigatans, 08003
apresski.es

①
La Botiga del Primavera Sound, El Born
Record industry

One of Barcelona's most renowned summer festivals – Primavera Sound (*see page 83*) – also has its own record label and shop. The endeavour is testament to Primavera's independent spirit, which defends the grassroots music scene by programming a third of the festival billing with up-and-coming Spanish artists. It also often signs them to the festival's eponymous label (El Segell del Primavera), which keeps their sounds spinning across the world all year round.
1 Carrer dels Ases, 08003
+34 93 624 2915
primaverasound.es

**② **
La Central, Dreta de l'Eixample
Targeted tomes

Antonio Ramírez opened his first bookshop as a medium-sized seller that retained the intimate, personalised service of an independent. La Central is now a national success story, present in several locations in Barcelona and Madrid and offering titles inside premiere artistic institutions such as Muhba.

Staff personally manage specific sections according to the tastes of the community. So while blockbuster titles are given shelf space, they're not placed on a pedestal. "A good bookshop should never simply try to sell a lot of copies of only a few titles," says Ramírez.
237 Carrer de Mallorca, 08008
+34 90 080 2109
lacentral.com

③
Malpaso Librería, Dreta de
l'Eixample
Volume control

Confident and cool, Malpaso
is the extension of the similarly
named publishing house formed
by enterprising Mexicans in
2013. The bookshop and
adjoining Mexican restaurant
opened three years later. "The
idea was to reclaim the idea of
the neighbourhood bookshop,"
says manager Bernat Colomer.
  Titles are organised
according to small publishers,
giving avid readers an insight
into the breadth of each house's
work. The dynamic space also
hosts regular exhibitions on the
split level upstairs and invites
prominent guests to curate
special sections on topics
and themes such as Russian
literature and the universe.
*331 Carrer de la Diputació, 08009
+34 93 018 5732
malpasolibreria.com*

Three more bookshops

01 Llibrería Sant
    Jordi, Barri Gòtic:
    A mouthwatering mixture
    of some 6,000 books
    about art, design and
    photography is crammed
    into this one-time
    potpourri shop. "The
    only thing we don't stock
    is poor taste," says owner
    Josep Morales.
    llibreriasantjordi.com

02 Múltiplos, El Raval:
    A stone's throw from
    Macba's contemporary
    art, this small bookshop
    stocks art-themed titles
    and focuses on Spanish,
    Portuguese and Latin
    American publications.
    multiplosbooks.org

03 COAC, Barri Gòtic:
    Catalonia's College of
    Architects, which goes by
    the acronym COAC, has
    one of Barcelona's most
    extensive anthologies of
    architecture and design
    books, nestled alongside
    its equally impressive
    lower-level gift shop.
    arquitectes.cat

**Discos Paradiso,
El Raval**
—

Some of the world's most
recognisable DJs are loyal
customers here. Arnau Ferré
and Gerard López house new
releases in the front and vintage
at the back, and carry the best
electronica titles in town.
discosparadiso.com

Things we'd buy
—— In the bag

Now that we've pointed out our favourite shops we're going to suggest what to squeeze into that extra suitcase. Barcelona has long had a vibrant design scene so you'll find plenty to choose from.

We've eschewed the gift-shop tat for tasteful trinkets: think Santa & Cole's cosy Cestita lamp, colourful and quintessentially Mediterranean ceramics, well-wrought leather goods from talented young designers and a print by one of Barcelona's greatest artists. To stave off those post-holiday blues we've also rounded up the flavours we're most fond of, from bomba rice and artisanal chocolate to crisp orange wine and *vermut*. Plenty to keep you well stocked until your next visit.

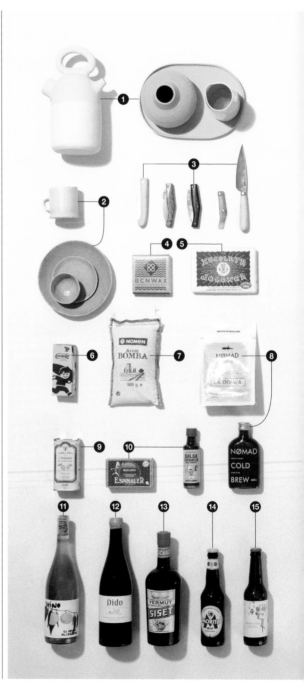

01 Ceramics by Working in
the Redwoods
workingintheredwoods.com
02 Nonabruna ceramics from
Moritz Store *moritz.com*
03 Pallarès knives from Mica
mica.barcelona
04 BCN Wax surf wax from Box
Barcelona *boxbarcelona.com*
05 Jolonch chocolate from
Vicens *vicens.com*
06 Cacaolat chocolate milk from
El Corte Inglés *elcorteingles.es*
07 Nomen bomba rice from
Jespac *jespac.com*
08 Coffee beans and cold
brew by Nømad Coffee
nomadcoffee.es
09 Azada lemon-and-olive oil
from Colmado Casa Buendía
+34 93 463 8701
10 Espinaler tinned mussels
and salsa from Vila Viniteca
vilaviniteca.es
11 Orange wine by Casa Bonay
casabonay.com
12 Dido red wine by Venus
La Universal from La Vinícola
lavinicola.cat
13 Siset vermut from Colmado
Quilez *lafuente.es*
14 Beer by Moritz *moritz.com*
15 Roses de Llobregat IPA from
Entre Latas *entrelatas-bcn.com*
16 Scissors, pen and tray by
Doiy *doiydesign.com*
17 Woouf notebook from OMG
BCN *omgbcn.com*
18 Colouring pencils by Museu
Picasso *museupicasso.bcn.cat*
19 Octaevo notebook and
bookmarks from OMG BCN
omgbcn.com
20 Mario Ruiz minihouses from
Macba *macba.cat*
21 Gaudí paving stone from
Casa Milà *store.lapedrera.com*
22 Passeig de Gràcia stone tile
by Solnhofen *solnhofen.es*
23 Leather clutch by Iriarte
Iriarte *iriarteiriarte.com*
24 Kaleos sunglasses from
Sueños Negros *suneonline.com*
25 *Joan Miró: The Ladder of
Escape* by Fundació Joan Miró
fmirobcn.org

26 Ölend backpack from Be
Bonavista *bethestore.com*
27 Miguel Milá's Cestita lamp
by Santa & Cole from Espai Rö
espairo.com
28 Octaevo paper vase from OMG
BCN *omgbcn.com*
29 Batabasta cushion from Casa
Bonay *casabonay.com*
30 Teixidors throw from Bel y Cia
belycia.com

31 Swimming trunks by Brava
Fabrics
bravafabrics.com
32 *Homage to Catalonia* by
George Orwell from La Central
lacentral.com
33 Joan Brossa print by
Fundació Joan Brossa
fundaciojoanbrossa.cat
34 Espadrilles by The Rice Co
thericeco.com

12 essays
—— Musings
on Barcelona

*I think I'm
ready for
something
a little less
horticultural...*

*Cultivo
de
Rosas*

ESSAY 01
Culture factory
Industrial legacy
___

Buildings that tell the
story of the Catalan
capital's industrial past
have been saved from the
wrecking ball and now
play a big part in the
city's cultural life.

*by Marta Puigdemasa,
writer*

Sun, sea, sand, Gaudí and tapas. If you
were to imagine a list of words that a visitor
might reasonably associate with Barcelona,
these would likely top it – and I'm willing
to bet that the word "industry" would be
nowhere to be seen. Few people know that
in the 18th and 19th centuries this "design
capital" was, in fact, the "locomotive
of Spain".

The first textile factories opened in
the 1730s in meadows that today form the
neighbourhoods of El Raval and Sant Pere
(also known as El Born); they soon spread
to the city's peripheries, including Sant
Andreu, Sants and Sant Martí, where
chimneys sprouted like mushrooms. The
latter became "Barcelona's workshop",
with the *barri* of Poblenou as its engine.

Although they often go unnoticed, the
vestiges of Barcelona's industrial past still
very much exist and you don't need to be
Sherlock Holmes to find them. You might
spot them in a street name, an unusual
structure or an anachronistic touch on
a façade. A century ago, central locations

such as La Rambla, Avinguda de Roma
and Carrer de Mallorca housed many
factories and industrial units. The
Fundació Antoni Tàpies, today a
contemporary-art museum, used
to be a publishing house. Popular
restaurant El Nacional on Passeig de
Gràcia was a dye manufacturer and the
Hiroshima theatre, renowned for its
unconventional performances, once
made lifts and escalators.

The oil crisis of 1973 caused many
industries to leave the city in search of
cheaper land. Others simply closed down,
leaving hundreds of industrial buildings
to the cobwebs and the wrecking ball;
in the run up to the 1992 Summer
Olympics the latter was having a field
day. Most of them would have been
turned to dust had it not been for the
locals, who fought to save the buildings
and convert them into public spaces.

Thanks to them, today the Vapor
Vell factory in Sant Andreu is a library,
while Ca l'Aranyó, a former cotton
producer, is a
university campus
building. Can
Fabra is a cultural
centre and the
brick building
across the street,
a spinning mill
in years past,
houses Fabra i
Coats (*see page
137*): an enormous
contemporary-art museum, cultural
space and artists' residency.

> *"The vestiges
> of Barcelona's
> industrial past
> still very much
> exist and you
> don't need to
> be Sherlock
> Holmes to
> find them"*

In Poblenou – a poster child of
"industrial rejuvenation" and where I
once lived in a former button factory
– the transformation started in 2000 under
the government-sponsored project 22@.
Its objective was to convert the *barri*
into Catalonia's own Silicon Valley but
cultural and creative entities played –
and continue to play – a huge role in the
area's metamorphosis. It's home to the
HQ of the Sónar music festival, Vice Spain

and myriad advertising agencies, film producers and design studios. What's more, many of the loft spaces in the old factories and warehouses have been converted into live-work studios for artists, artisans and other creatives. Culture has given industry a new lease of life.

An icon of this movement, whose history is steeped in romance and which I encourage everyone to visit, is the Fábrica Lehmann at 159 Consell de Cent in the middle of Eixample. In 1894 a couple from Nuremburg arrived in Barcelona for their honeymoon. They instantly fell in love with the city and decided to open a second outpost for their German toy-making business here. For years they produced porcelain dolls under the brand name Eden-Bebé, which I'm told were the most sought-after in Spain at the time. But with the advent of the Spanish Civil War in 1936 the factory went from fashioning dolls to producing cutlery for the republican army. After the conflict the building was carved up into small mechanics' workshops, warehouses, offices and printing presses.

Today, if you enter the courtyard through the main cobbled passageway, you'll find that though the 25-metre-high chimney that once exuded the smoke from the fired porcelain is still in place, the factory workers have been succeeded by artists, photographers, editorial offices and fashion designers such as Josep Abril. There's even a pop-up restaurant called Rooftop Smokehouse.

The structure that perhaps best encapsulates the transformation of Barcelona's industrial landscape is the old Sansón cement factory in Sant Just Desvern on the city's outskirts. In 1973 the architect Ricardo Bofill transformed some 5,000 sq m of dust and concrete into his home and office, naming it La Fábrica (*see page 117*) in homage to its past. It's a place that he still calls home to this day.

Waking up in such a building every morning must be like travelling back to the very origins of Catalonia's industrial revolution. Interestingly, the building's form doesn't follow its function, but in Bofill's eyes not everything has to be as it appears. Towering, ivy-clad concrete walls can just as easily house a prestigious architectural practice, complete with exquisite furniture, as anything else. Why? Because the true wealth of this factory-cathedral isn't in the tastefully added, modest materials or the minimalist decor but rather in the space itself. Its magnificence was always there; it simply had to be uncovered.

It seems that today's culture has come to understand and recognise the unique spaces that lie dormant within these industrial vestiges, waiting for a second chance. — (M)

Tasty repurposed buildings
—
01 Espacio 88
An impressive architecture studio and cafeteria.
02 Fábrica Moritz
Restored 19th-century brewery.
03 Sopa
Vegetarian restaurant in the heart of industrial Poblenou.

ABOUT THE WRITER: Marta Puigdemasa is a writer and editor focusing on social, cultural and technology literature. She's also the founder of *Perdiz*, a magazine on happiness.

ESSAY 02
Something fishy
Catalan cuisine

———

Catalonia's kitchens are good for more than just tapas. Step away from the small plates and instead try the regional speciality that spices up pieces of meat with... fish.

by Carlos Román Alcaide, writer

It may not strike *you* as weird but it certainly did me: meatballs and calamari, really? Coming from Seville, where surf'n'turf doesn't often find its way onto the menu, I was bemused. However, one bite was all it took to convince me that these people knew what they were doing.

Before we go into the origins of *mar i muntanya* – literally "sea and mountain" – cuisine, it helps to understand a little about Catalonia's geography. To the north lie France, Andorra and the the Pyrenees, while to the south you'll find Valencia and, to the west, the province of Aragón. The east belongs exclusively to the Mediterranean Sea, which has formed the essence of Catalan (and Valencian) cuisine for centuries, providing the region with countless varieties of fish, seafood and edible plants. The territory inland, on the other hand, is a veritable mosaic: the rich and fertile fields of Lleida, the rice fields of Tarragona and the semi-rocky landscape of Girona.

So where does the tradition of *mar i muntanya* come from? There are several theories but one of the most reliable traces its origins to *De Re Coquinaria* (*On Culinary Matters*), a book of sumptuous Roman recipes that's some 2,000 years old. Among its pages you'll find a cornucopia of exotic dishes, including a kind of dessert that consists of meat and fish. If we take into account the fact that the Romans had a strong presence on the Iberian Peninsula, including what is now Girona's Empordà region, as well as a will to expand their culture wherever they went, it makes sense that they would take their recipes with them.

Another popular legend traces the origins of *mar i muntanya* to Girona, some centuries later. It's said that a *pagesa* (Catalan peasant woman) from Empordà came up with a recipe consisting of chicken and lobster. Lobster was not the delicacy it is today; it was simply another typical ingredient hauled in by the region's fishermen. The reason behind the unlikely combination was simple: she didn't have enough lobster for the dish so she went to the yard and killed a couple of chickens. Regardless of its accuracy there's no doubt that it shows a common trend ubiquitous in every culture and every century: the average person had to make do with whatever the soil (or sea) provided.

Over time, the concept of *mar i muntanya* found its place among the most popular and exemplary recipes of Catalonia's cuisine. Such is its influence over the region's culture that it was one of the first recipes I learned when I was studying to become a chef. It also led me to discover and taste countless delicious dishes: *mandonguilles amb sípia* (those meatballs with calamari), *pollastre de pagès amb bolets i gambes* (a stew of chicken with mushrooms and prawns) and, one of the wildest combinations and a personal favourite of mine, *peus de porc amb escamarlans* (pig trotters with scampi).

"Every time someone asks me for a good paella or tapas restaurant I tell them that Catalan cuisine is so much more than that"

Every time someone asks me for a good paella or tapas restaurant in Barcelona, I give them a few recommendations. But I also tell them that Catalan cuisine is so much more than that. I tell them about the beautiful contrast between textures and flavours of *mar i muntanya*, about the importance of such dishes in the region's culture and their embodiment of Catalonia's terroir. When you find yourself in Barcelona, give the chicken and lobster a go – I promise it won't disappoint. — (M)

Top spots for 'mar i muntanya'
—
01 **La Pubilla**
Simple barstool dining in Gràcia.
02 **Sergi de Meià**
Try the pig trotter and scampi melange.
03 **Manairó**
A swanky take by chef Jordi Herrera.

ABOUT THE WRITER: Carlos Román Alcaide is the creator and co-director of food project No Más de Mamá. He has since worked for the likes of *El Comidista* and *PlayGround Food*, where he was editor in chief.

ESSAY 03

Keeping up with the Catalans
Home truths

Tune in to hear the contradictory statements spouted daily from the lips of Barcelona's proud residents – and how to handle them.

by Liam Aldous,
Monocle

"This is the best city in the world." So says pretty much every Barcelona resident within minutes of meeting you. Later that same person may complain about the maladies of mass tourism, seemingly unperturbed by the connection between their own puffy-chested promotion and the upsurge of travellers who flock to their shores. This is your first brush with one of the many contradictions inherent to the Catalan character.

Affluent yet parsimonious, pragmatic with a tendency to dream big and proudly international but instinctively insular: the Catalan superiority complex is matched only by a proclivity for self-defensiveness. But such endless dichotomies, rather than detracting from the Catalan character, are the colour of daily life. In a country as diverse as Spain, resorting to lighthearted regional stereotypes is a national sport. Feeding a stream of fun-loving jokes, these caricatures also act as a guide to the social idiosyncrasies that dot the Iberian Peninsula. Spaniards may laugh about Catalonia's love of *gafapasta* (expensive eyewear) but this is a mask for their respect for (and envy of) the region's pioneering spirit. A spirit embellished in Gaudí's edifices, made edible by maestros of modern Catalan cuisine such as Ferran Adrià and embodied by FC Barcelona's foot soldiers.

As would be expected of such a paradoxical region there's a puerile side that undermines the elegance and entrepreneurship, such as the prevalence of poo-related traditions. It's the fault of the caganers – small squatting figurines politely doing their business – placed within a miniature nativity scene. Purists claim it's a holy act of fertilising sacred ground but with a number of caganers being made in the form of celebrities and politicians, others smirk about its power as a levelling device: an act of defecation that cuts the mighty down to size.

Scatological humour aside, one thing you'll notice about the Catalans is their solidarity, best embodied by *castells*, a sport that involves the construction of human towers. In Barcelona this shoulder-to-shoulder spirit has spurred many organised rebellions, earning the city the epithet *la rosa de foc* (the rose of fire). When former activist Ada Colau became the city's first female mayor in 2015 she said, "There aren't many other cities that would elect someone like me". But therein lines another enigma. Catalans often claim to be a bastion of left-leaning idealists, "the Denmark of the south". What they don't mention is that the same centre-right party has governed more or less continuously since the dawn of Spanish democracy in 1977. In the controversial 2017 election the two parties with the most votes were Ciutadans and Junts per Catalunya – both lean to the right.

> *"What locals don't mention is that the same centre-right party has governed more or less since the dawn of Spanish democracy"*

Catalans may be socially progressive but, when it comes to voting, the majority still tend to tick conservative.

Catalan author Josep Pla mused on their "irreducible duality", which he said stemmed from a fear of being oneself. "The Catalan is a fugitive," he wrote, "fleeing from both himself and others… sometimes he is a lackey, at others an insurgent. Sometimes a conformist, then a rebel… even when a Catalan attacks he is on the defensive." Which brings us to the last paradox. Any utterance of a cheeky, unerring observation (much like those outlined here) runs the risk of provoking charges of *Catalanofobia*: a defensive term usually aimed at anyone perceived to be hostile to Catalan culture, traditions or the nationalist secessionist drive.

Never fear: as proud as they are, most Catalans are still pushovers for a compliment (and have plenty to be proud of), so simply lay on the charm, admire their singular achievements and you'll win them over. And, if you're still clutching for some foolproof flattery, you can always look your Catalan counterpart in the eye and concede: "Yes, Barcelona really is the best city in the world." — (M)

Catalan quirks
——
01 Not so Gothic Quarter
The so-called Barri Gotic was in fact embellished in the 20th C.
02 Tió de Nadal
The "poo log" that sits under Catalan Christmas trees.
03 'Closer to Europe'
A claim to be "more European", evident in the use of *mercès* in lieu of *gràcies*.

ABOUT THE WRITER: Since 2011, Liam Aldous has been MONOCLE's Madrid correspondent, travelling to Catalonia on an almost monthly basis. He watches the rivalry between his adopted city and Barcelona with bemusement.

The magic of 'el disseny'
Barcelona's design heyday

In the run-up to the 1992 Olympics the design world caught a whiff of something happening in the Catalan capital. It was the dawn of a new age of creativity in Barcelona. But is it all just a memory?

by Begoña Gómez Urzaiz, writer

In March 1988, Barcelona's mayor Pasqual Maragall took a seat in the Fundació Joan Miró, a stone's throw from what would become the Palau Sant Jordi stadium. To his left was Josep Maria Trias, who was about to present his logo for the 1992 Summer Olympics. It was a human figure painted in three strokes that resembled the logo of La Caixa bank, designed in 1980 by Joan Miró himself. To Maragall's right was Javier Mariscal, famous among the underground design crowd for his outlandish furniture and obscene comics.

Mariscal was responsible for designing the mascot Cobi, based on a herding dog like those found in the Pyrenees. Cobi was different to his predecessors: the tiger of Seoul 1988, for example, or eagle Sam of Los Angeles 1984. Cobi didn't descend from a Disney or Asian animation tradition; he had sharp corners and was hard to reproduce in toy format. But he was new and eye-catching, a mascot for a newly modern Barcelona as well as for the Olympics, so Mariscal won the day.

The public was split into those who "got" Cobi and those who didn't. No one really wanted to belong to the latter camp as it implied that you were a bit "square" – someone who wasn't ready for the modern Barcelona, which was being ushered into the new era with an explosion of design to complement its novel image.

But this design culture didn't come from nowhere. The city has a long creative tradition, nurtured in art schools such as EINA and Escola Massana, and a pantheon of world-renowned architects. So when Barcelona fell into this Olympic design frenzy it created a forum of expression not only for veteran designers such as André Ricard, who designed the Olympic torch, but also for an emergent generation.

The new movement, however, flourished not in schools but "design bars". These were a handful of new hangouts with names such as Velvet and Nick Havanna, where you would find América Sánchez, Pedro Pubill Calaf (known as Peret), Enric Satué and none other than Mariscal himself, who became the epitome of *el diseñador* (the designer) perched on the famously uncomfortable bar stools. What they all had in common was a certain joie de vivre in their approach. And how could they not be cheerful? For the first time they were overwhelmed with commissions, well paid and, most importantly, able to justify to their mothers why they hadn't gone into law or finance.

Europe descended on Barcelona to see what on earth was happening. And what did they discover? *El disseny*, the new Catalan design tradition. It was woven into the fabric of the city. There were shops such as Vinçon, which sold radio transistors alongside Varius chairs by Oscar Tusquets, furniture-makers Santa & Cole and BD, and magazines *De Diseño* and

> *"The city has a long creative tradition and a pantheon of world-renowned architects"*

Ardi. El disseny had gripped every corner of the city, from the wealthy boulevards of Eixample down to the humblest streets of El Raval. Companies paid graphic designers handsome sums to revamp their image and every neighbourhood bar redesigned its menu with something a little more colourful and fun. The result wasn't always great but, as with the Olympics, what mattered was the taking part.

In 2015, Vinçon closed down; today it's a gigantic Massimo Dutti. That same year Mariscal, who had spent two decades doing everything from animating films to designing hotels, went bankrupt. A pessimist would read this as the demise of *el disseny* but the optimist would find reasons to be cheerful all the same. Once a month Palo Alto Market, the creative compound where Mariscal's studio was based, hosts a market where young graphic, furniture and fashion designers gather to promote their work, sell their goods and hone their entrepreneurial skills. Their audience, which packs out the complex, still appreciates a little quirkiness in design. After all, they grew up with Cobi. — (M)

Barcelona street sculptures
—

01 'Gambrinus' (1992)
A huge lobster by Mariscal.
02 'Dona i Ocell' (1983)
Some 22 metres of vivid colour by Joan Miró.
03 'Tribute to Picasso' (1981 to 1983)
Antoni Tàpies' furniture in a glass box.

ABOUT THE WRITER: Begoña Gómez Urzaiz is a writer living in Barcelona. She writes for *La Vanguardia, El País, Icon, S Moda* and *Dazed & Confused* and lives by the old Nora Ephron motto: "Everything is copy".

ESSAY 05
The wisdom of parrots
An avian encounter
———
Humans aren't the only ones who've been seduced by Barcelona's charms. In this fictional short story, a visitor's future is decided when he's transfixed by a flock of exotic birds.

by Inma Buendía, writer

I woke up with the first rays of light filtering into my new home. Two days earlier I had moved to Barcelona, where I intended to spend at least a year, a 12-month sabbatical from my life in London. So here I was, in the centre of El Born, on a narrow street just like the ones I had dreamed of while reading the novels of Carlos Ruiz Zafón: small alleyways with close-knit cobblestones, home to speakeasies and shops selling spices in bulk. Impatient to unravel and document all the mysteries of my new city, I raced out onto the street with my camera.

However, just as I lined up my first shot, a loud noise took me by surprise. I had never heard anything like it: a cloud of parrots singing thunderously all at once, as though in dialogue with one another, oblivious to the morning silence of a city still soundly asleep.

I instinctively followed them, eager to know what they were saying, where they had come from and where they were headed. I crossed Passeig de Picasso without looking, narrowly avoiding a taxi, my eyes firmly fixed on the sky.

I've always been fond of birds, perhaps because they symbolise the total liberty that I've long sought myself. Until that point I had done everything that was expected of me: I studied business, secured a good job and got married. Everything was fine until a long-suppressed desire to escape had driven me to take a break.

Finally the birds stopped flying; they arrived at what appeared to be some sort of abandoned greenhouse, slap bang in the centre of Parc de la Ciutadella, full of junk and plants that snaked around shards of broken glass. I must have looked completely bewildered because an old man approached me and asked whether I was alright. I told him I was fine, all the while keeping my eyes on the ceiling. Reading my thoughts, he started telling me about the birds.

The monk parakeet, he said, is a species of parrot originally from Argentina that lives in the palm trees and rooftops of Barcelona. An estimated 5,000 live across the city. He remembered vividly how the petite parrots, following the

discovery of the first nest in 1975, spread across Barcelona. "No one knows how this species arrived in our city," he said. "They may have been pets that were set free or perhaps they arrived by ship and, enticed by the warm climate and exotic parks, decided to stay."

I retrieved my camera and started taking pictures. Their beaks and plumage were varied but unanimously beautiful, bathed in neverending shades of green, yellow and blue. On returning home I was able to think of little else; the image of the parrots had stuck fast in my mind. I remembered what my mother used to say to me: "Your head is always in the clouds. One of these days you'll fly away." Maybe the birds were some sort of sign.

"The parrots all live here in harmony, feeding on a colourful feast of dates, hackberries, eucalyptus leaves and cypress berries"

I scoured the internet and learned that the monk parakeet, though the most numerous, is not the only species of parrot in Barcelona. Another six had been discovered: Nanday, rose-ringed, blue-headed, mitred, red-masked and Senegal. They all live here in harmony, feeding on a colourful feast of dates, hackberries, eucalyptus leaves and cypress berries.

A year later I revisited the greenhouse. My sabbatical was over and it was time to make a decision: should I return to London? The parrots had doubled in number; clearly they had decided that Barcelona wasn't a bad place to build a nest. And I realised that I didn't want to renounce the wings that this city had given me either. Never had I been happier.

I didn't go back to London; I quit my old job for good and bid farewell to my wife, whom I certainly didn't deserve. Every year I return to the greenhouse, sit down and watch the parrots, remembering how they taught me that you don't really need wings to take flight. — (M)

> **Parrots by numbers**
> ——
> 01 **Now**
> There are thought to be about 10,000 in the city.
> 02 **Then**
> On arrival in 1975 there were fewer than 100.
> 03 **In flight**
> They tend to travel in flocks of 30 to 50.

ABOUT THE WRITER: Inma Buendia is a Basque journalist who has lived in Barcelona for seven years. She writes for *Openhouse* magazine and handles the press and communications for several cultural projects.

ESSAY 06
Street smarts
Dress to impress
——
The pride of Barcelonans is nowhere more evident than in Gràcia's annual best-dressed street competition – featuring a hot-air balloon, surf boards and much, much more.

by Raphael Minder, writer

Every August the district of Gràcia holds a week-long celebration in which residents compete to create the best-decorated street. Each one selects a different theme: in 2016 one thoroughfare was transformed into a series of textile workshops, echoing the industrial might of fin de siècle Barcelona; on Carrer de Verdi there was a Californian theme. The lion emblem of the Metro-Goldwyn-Mayer studios crowned an arch and the pavements boasted a version of the Hollywood Walk of Fame, studded with stars that each bore the name of a Gràcia street. Further down the road, Californian surfboards hung overhead. It may sound complicated but residents dress their streets with great inventiveness and economy. For instance, the mighty roaring lion of MGM was made with chicken wire and covered in painted newspaper.

Other streets sought literary inspiration. On Travessia de Sant Antoni, for instance, residents made decorations inspired by the novels of Jules Verne, with a replica of a hot-air balloon and a bar in the shape of Captain Nemo's *Nautilus* submarine.

Such celebrations date back to 1817, when Gràcia was still a separate town to Barcelona. Though it was incorporated into the fast-expanding city in 1897, it has retained its "small town" atmosphere. Today the festivities attract thousands of Catalans and hordes of summertime tourists. The festivities receive some public subsidies but what makes them special is that they're entirely managed by residents, who celebrate the event with an enormous alfresco dinner served on tables running down the centre of their street.

"Everybody comes to look at the street decorations but the most important part of the event is what happens before, when people come together to make all this happen," says Dolors Martínez, a feisty member of the Verdi association who has always lived in Gràcia. "This is all about having a relationship with many people who share a single passion: our Gràcia."

The Verdi association's 90 members each pay an annual fee of €50 but more

"Organisers take particular pride in the fact that they don't rely on the funding and logistical support of politicians to run their festivities"

volunteers and entire families join them to help during the celebrations. The children of Gràcia play a big part. Ten-year-old Artur Panasiouk wore an oversized devil's head during a street parade of *gegants* (giant statues). At home he collects miniature versions of these gargantuan effigies. "Some kids play video games but Artur much prefers our giants," says his mother.

Fiestas are common in nearly every town across Spain, particularly during the summer. In many places they're treated almost as a pilgrimage, with city-dwellers returning for a few days or weeks to the village where they grew up and catching up with childhood friends.

The main annual festival of Barcelona is a much larger affair. Known as La Mercè, or Our Lady of Mercy, it has taken place since the 17th century, when authorities crowned the Virgin the patroness of Barcelona and held celebrations to thank her for helping the city fight off a plague of locusts.

Officially held on 24 September, La Mercè is in fact a week-long festival. It showcases Catalan culture and traditions in dozens of separate events across the city, including nightly open-air concerts and the formation of several *castells* (human towers), which are topped by a small child. Another highlight of La Mercè is the fireworks and music show held at the water fountains of Montjuïc Park.

At a time of territorial tensions between Madrid and Barcelona over the question of Catalan independence, locals have also been focusing intensely on the *pregó* (official speech) that opens the festivities of La Mercè and is traditionally delivered by a writer or philosopher chosen by Barcelona's city hall. In 2017 philosopher Marina Garcés used the inaugural speech to criticise political attempts to turn Barcelona into a "Mediterranean Manhattan" or a theme park. At a time when separatists were hoping to convert Barcelona into the capital of a new Catalan republic, she also recalled the anarchist and "anti-authoritarian" spirit of the city in the 1930s, saying that Barcelona was a "free woman" and a "princess who has no desire for a kingdom or a husband".

For better or worse, such political undertones will always exist in these exuberant, ancient celebrations. The same spirit of independence dominates the celebrations in Gràcia, whose organisers take particular pride in the fact that they don't rely on the funding and logistical support of politicians to run their festivities, which is the norm in most Spanish towns.

Nonetheless, politics or not, this is a time when communities truly come together, forget their differences, and embrace their neighbours, no matter the street from which they hail.

As he gazes over his crowded street, Sergi Font, the president of the Verdi association, acknowledges that it can all come across as a little chaotic. "But," he says, "this is really the result of great neighbourhood cohesion, of many months of working together." — (M)

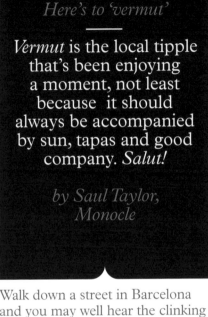

ESSAY 07

Herbal remedy
Here's to 'vermut'

Vermut is the local tipple that's been enjoying a moment, not least because it should always be accompanied by sun, tapas and good company. *Salut!*

by *Saul Taylor,*
Monocle

More Barcelona festivities
——
01 Rambla-Festes del Roser
A celebration of craftsmanship along La Rambla.
02 Festa Major de Sants
Eight days of concerts, dancing and street parties.
03 Festes de Santa Eulàlia
Honouring the city's patron saint.

ABOUT THE WRITER: Raphael Minder is the Spain and Portugal correspondent for *The New York Times*, as well as the author of *The Struggle for Catalonia: Rebel Politics in Spain.*

Walk down a street in Barcelona and you may well hear the clinking of bottles. But this isn't simply another morning-after trudge to the recycling station or the delivery of crates of Estrella Damm to a neighbourhood bar. Instead this has the timbre of someone on their merry way to refill their glass flagons with wine and *vermut*.

A local variation of the classic vermouth – the fortified wine flavoured with botanicals that has enjoyed something of a renaissance with the reappearance of the Martini and Negroni on cocktail menus across the globe – *vermut* is a perennial ritual in Barcelona. As in Italy, aperitivo (or *aperitiu* in Catalan) is a sacred tradition in Spain in which the appetite is whetted before lunch and dinner with light bites and a glass of something giddy. Served over ice in a tumbler, with a dash of soda from the *sifón* (siphon) and either a slice of orange or a shaving of its peel, *vermut* is more than just something to sip: it's a civilised moment in which to reflect and relax.

Spotting a *vermut* drinker is easy: they'll be sat angled towards the sun with legs outstretched, nonchalantly popping anchovy-stuffed olives into their mouths with their eyes closed while remaining completely engaged in conversation. *Vermut*'s alcoholic content, 5 or 6 per cent above wine, gives the drinker a mellow glow, and its bittersweet, herby aroma is the ideal foil for *patatas fritas* (chips) doused in Espinaler sauce, roasted almonds or small, deep-fried tapas.

Every bar in the city worth its salt will offer a handful of options to try but in general the *vermut de casa* will be more than adequate and, when a good slug of the brown stuff generally costs less than a freshly squeezed orange juice, who's complaining? Barcelona's best bars serve small *montaditos* – bruschetta-like snacks – as an accompaniment.

Classic spots such as Quimet i Quimet (*see page 39*) in Poble-sec or Cal Pep in Barceloneta are pretty much unbeatable for both food and drink. But if you'd rather forego the queues in favour of a seat and a conversation that you can actually hear, you can't go wrong with Betlem and nearby Café Búho in Eixample or Tarannà in Sant Antoni.

Rarely does a bottle of *vermut* exceed €10 but, considering the time and effort it takes to produce and the varying results of the process, it's worth finding a favourite. *Vermut* is made when a local wine variety, such as Macabeu, is left to ferment with yeast at a low temperature before being darkened, sometimes with green walnuts. The *vermut* is then macerated with local herbs that can include cloves, cinnamon, citrus peel, basil and thyme, before sitting in wood casks using the traditional system of *solera* (ageing and blending) for six months.

> "Spotting a 'vermut' drinker is easy: they'll be sat angled into the sun with legs outstretched, nonchalantly popping anchovy-stuffed olives into their mouths"

Start your *vermut* education at Colmado Casa Buendía in Eixample. Owner Susana Palomino has stocked her *colmado* (deli) with some of the finest local produce – from olive oil, tinned fish and jam to biscuits, wines and loose grains – and the *vermut* selection is a careful edit of Catalonia's best brewers.

Visitors to Buendía will inevitably leave with a hearty litre of Musugorri sold in traditional stoneware, a Casa Mariol with its beautiful inverted italic logo printed in white on its stout bottle, a jolly El Bandarra or an old-school red-labelled Rofes. However, the highlight of any visit is an impromptu tasting of the house variety, the Montseta Valls Vermut Negro. Palomino sells the stuff from large barrels and a steady stream of clients can be found on a Saturday before lunch, stockpiling for the weekend and stopping for a chat over a morsel of *torró* (nougat) while she fills their carafes.

Vermut represents the best of Barcelona: fierce pride, dedication to craft and independent production and, most importantly, any excuse to get gently sozzled in the sun with friends and family on a Saturday afternoon. — (M)

Where to buy 'vermut'

——

01 **Bar Electricitat**
Vermut and seafood is a match made in heaven.
02 **Morro Fi**
The bar serves its own *vermut*.
03 **Bodega Maestrazgo**
Old-school wine bar and tasting room.

ABOUT THE WRITER: Saul Taylor is a Barcelona-based writer and contributing editor at MONOCLE (he was once a section editor too). When he's not scribbling away he spends plenty of time in the Catalan sun with *vermut* in hand.

ESSAY 08

A ball on the beach
Primavera Sound

——

A beautiful setting, the best international and local bands, a friendly crowd and a comfy bed to go back to at the end of the night. Welcome to music-festival heaven.

*by Holly Fisher,
Monocle*

If you board a flight from London to Barcelona in late May you'll find an unexpected sense of camaraderie among passengers: most people on the plane are embarking on the same annual pilgrimage to a Spanish musical Mecca.

There are plenty of reasons to head to Barcelona for a long weekend but the Primavera Sound music festival is my favourite excuse for returning to the Catalan capital. Overlooking the Mediterranean in the former Olympic site of Parc del Fòrum, it has become one of the most renowned celebrations of music in Europe. As you wander from stage to stage through the Parc, clutching a cool beer, you'll meet good-looking crowds speaking every language imaginable. This fiesta has been attracting an international audience since 2001 and, with such vast and high-profile line-ups in a city that knows how to have a good time, why wouldn't it?

Despite the roster of global names on the schedule and the international nature of the audience, the folks behind Primavera have always been keen to keep the festival a Spanish affair. So while you can expect to find names such as Radiohead, Kendrick Lamar and LCD Soundsystem at the top of the bill, cast your gaze a little lower and you'll discover a wealth of local talent: about 30 per cent of performance slots are reserved for Spanish artists.

"We have a strong commitment to new bands and we try to give them the opportunity to play at a big festival; we want to be a window for Spanish bands looking to play to international audiences," says Aleix Ibars from the Primavera team. "We also spread the Primavera feeling during the whole month, with free shows in bars and cultural centres before the festival, as well as Primavera a la Ciutat at CCCB (*see page 95*), where we hold free shows during the festival weekend."

The Primavera brand has become engrained in the city. It hold events throughout the year, has its own record label (El Segell del Primavera) and even a record shop (*see page 64*). The festival site is littered with small stages showcasing Spanish artists, local labels sell records and T-shirts, and venues throughout the city put on their favourite bands.

"For a Brit like me, seeing thousands of Spanish gig-goers singing 'Tender' back to Blur by the beach is a wonderful thing"

Music festivals are a space for fun: inhibitions are lost, footwork gets fancier and you are far more likely to strike up a conversation with the person next to you than on your average night on the tiles. Attendees are united in their love of live music and Primavera is great for eclectic tastes. You might find Brian Wilson performing his *Pet Sounds* while John Carpenter plays *The Exorcist* theme tune nearby, and Arcade Fire pop up for a secret show. But the best thing about the festival – especially during a period of fractured nations, referendums and Brexit – is that the multilingual nature of the event makes it a place for everyone to get together and have a big old knees-up.

For a Brit like me, seeing thousands of Spanish gig-goers singing "Tender" back at Blur by the beach is a wonderful thing – and far greater than witnessing thousands of British people do the same in a muddy field in Somerset. To then amble around and discover a brilliant Basque or Catalan band makes you feel like you've made a fair trade in music.

It can be a struggle to feel proud about the UK these days but at Primavera you get a gentle reminder of the great exports from home, as well as a guide to the best bits of your host country. This is soft power in full swing: whether you're prancing around to a Spanish garage band, a Canadian art-pop group or a French electro star, everyone is having a grand time and getting along swimmingly.

Then there's the setting. The beach and the close proximity to the city centre are huge selling points. How nice it is to stroll down the coast or jump in a cab and roll into your hotel room at the end of the night rather than squelch back to a damp tent in a paddock. The site is far enough from residents for the party to last all night at full volume and close enough to get some sleep and a shower before it all starts again the next day. And if it works, keep doing it: Primavera has expanded to a sister festival in Porto too.

Are you sold? If so, you'll need to take a peculiarly Spanish approach to your day. The Primavera schedule requires lazy lunches on a *plaça* (square) – somewhere in Gràcia should be quiet enough to get over the previous night – and perhaps a short siesta during those mid-afternoon hours. Then a few drinks in El Raval and a quick study of the night's line-up before moving to Parc del Fòrum to let the games begin. This is a late-night festival so you'll be dancing from dusk till dawn.

The two main stages are opposite each other. Stand at one and catch PJ Harvey;

turn around to face the other and watch Air; look left and there's Barcelona; look right, there's the sea. But this isn't even the best bit. Back towards the entrance is everyone's favourite stage: the Ray Ban amphitheatre. It's here that the festival always draws to a close with Barcelona's DJ Coco, spinning dance and pop classics until the sun rises and everyone decamps to the beach.

When it comes to urban festivals, many places have tried to come up with a good formula but have been beset by noise restrictions, licensing problems and venue queues. Primavera, however, has nailed it: this festival is in tune with its city. — (M)

ESSAY 09
Walking the talk
Poetry on foot

———

How Barcelona resident and poet Joan Brossa gave a new meaning to poetry, using everything from clothes pegs to playing cards.

by Eloise Edgington, writer

Top three acts
——
01 Daphni (2013)
A dazzling electronica warm-up to DJ Coco's closing set.
02 LCD Soundsystem (2016)
All of the US electro band's European fans in one crowd.
03 Selda (2016)
At almost 70, the Turkish folk singer still draws big crowds.

ABOUT THE WRITER: Holly Fisher is senior radio producer at Monocle 24, specialising in the arts. Her Primavera recovery tips include ordering everything at Elephant, Crocodile, Monkey and nipping to Cadaqués for a siesta on the beach.

On 5 October 1979 a crowd gathered at Barcelona's Liceu theatre on La Rambla. A poetry festival was taking place and attendees had been invited to participate in a nocturnal tour of the city. The guide leading the tour was a resident of the Sarrià-Sant Gervasi neighbourhood: a poet and visual artist called Joan Brossa.

But a poet in the broadest sense of the word. His work came in the form of words, performances, installations and objects. The word "bilingualism" is often associated with Brossa, referring not to the ease with which he could shift from one language to another but to how he pushed the limits of language and expressed himself through objects and images as well as words.

That night's excursion, part of the Festa de la Lletra (Festival of Literature), was no run-of-the-mill city tour. It was one of Brossa's unique performance pieces, one which would later lead him to be considered a precursor of the anti-tourism movement that thrives in present-day Barcelona.

Born in 1919 in Carrer de Wagner, Brossa's work bore a deeply socio-political aspect, often rooted in both the local community and wider city. Barcelona was a source of inspiration throughout. He used his Brossian language as a form of activism, writing in Catalan when Catalan had been outlawed by the Franco dictatorship. His "object poetry" transformed everyday objects into works of art. Lightbulbs, playing cards, clothes pegs, toilet paper and potatoes were deformed or positioned to become satirical visual metaphors.

Brossa loved to walk. He said that to discover unfamiliar places you had to take unfamiliar routes. Conscious of the stifling impact that tourism was having on the city he mapped out a route off the well-trodden track so that his nocturnal companions might experience a more authentic Barcelona, one that you couldn't get to know through brochures or pamphlets but rather by fully engaging with the city.

He took his audience to businesses that had survived the passage of time. Among them was El Ingenio, a family workshop dating back to 1838 that sculpted the oversized papier-mâché heads and garish costumes of the *gegants* (*see page 80*). They swung by the city's oldest magic shop, El Rei de la Màgia, and stopped off at a dog shelter and a fakir performance, before ending up in França station to watch a striptease.

This route reflects the meandering challenge of seeking out Joan Brossa's own work around the city. Five years after the Festa de la Lletra took place, Brossa began to contribute to Barcelona's collection of public art. In 1984 he was commissioned to create a piece in the gardens of the cyclist Marià Cañardo. He created a "traversable visual poem in three parts: birth, journey – with pauses and intonations – and destruction". The work is a voyage in itself. At the start, a capital letter "A" stands almost 12 metres high and, along the way, punctuation marks are strewn across the grass. At the end the "A" is found in ruins, a symbol of death and devastation.

Brossa's poetry can be seen around Barcelona in squares, on

> *"Lightbulbs, playing cards, clothes pegs, toilet paper and potatoes were deformed or positioned to become satirical visual metaphors"*

buildings, down streets and in gardens. A mask-shaped plaque is embedded in the pavement of La Rambla. A homage to the book stands at the busy junction between Gran Via and Passeig de Gràcia. In Plaça Nova, in Barcelona's Barri Gòtic, seven sculptures spell out "Bàrcino" – the Roman name of Barcelona – in front of what remains of the Roman city wall.

You might stumble across Brossa's work near a well-known landmark, while other pieces must be actively sought out. You have to look hard to see what Brossa had to say, and perhaps venture down an unfamiliar street. But that's exactly what he would have wanted. — (M)

Brossa's life
—

01 **1936**
Joins the Republicans in the Spanish civil war.
02 **1948**
Founds surrealist magazine *Dau al Set*.
03 **1951**
Publishes his first collection of experimental poems.

ABOUT THE WRITER: Eloise Edgington is a British writer and editorial co-ordinator for PlayGround + video. She lives in Barcelona and has written for publications such as *Hunger Magazine* and *Metal Magazine*.

ESSAY 10
Sporting legend
The pride of Barcelona
—

A symbol of Catalan identity, a two-fingered gesture to Franco and a source of deep pride, FC Barcelona has always been true to its own motto: "more than a club".

by Melkon Charchoglyan, Monocle

I took my seat in the upper tiers of the Camp Nou and looked around, admiring a stadium that fills with about 100,000 fans come match day. There were plenty of youngsters in claret-coloured Barcelona tops, rubbing their hands together to stave off the evening chill, but equally numerous were the older gentlemen in their smart jackets and hats. All sported a lapel pin depicting the FC Barcelona crest: the flag of the patron saint of Catalonia, Sant Jordi (Saint George); the yellow-red *Senyera* ("the standard" in Catalan); and a football over the blue-and-claret-striped team strip.

The atmosphere was a cross between a rowdy weekend get-together and serious parliament session. The crowd chatted in Catalan for a few minutes and then burst into song:

Tant se val d'on venim
si del sud o del nord
ara estem d'acord, estem d'acord,
una bandera ens agermana.

"It doesn't matter where we come from / south or north," the club anthem goes. "Now we're all as one / united under a single flag." Whether you were born and bred in Eixample or hail from a tiny village 100km from Barcelona, here we're all as one. Here we're Catalan. The east stand of the stadium is emblazoned with the words "*més que un club*" (more than a club). And rightly so. Futbol Club Barcelona, or Barça for short, has always been the unofficial theatre of Catalan politics, pride and identity. Even its history is steeped in legend.

The club was founded in 1899 by Swiss footballer and entrepreneur Hans Gamper; on his way to Africa, he stopped in Barcelona to visit his uncle and was so taken with the city that he never left. On 22 October 1899 he took out a newspaper advert asking if anyone wanted to join him in establishing a football club – and the rest is history. He even changed his first name to Joan, which is typically Catalan.

> "*Whether you were born and bred in Eixample or hail from a tiny village 100km from Barcelona, here we're all as one. Here we're Catalan*"

There's no doubt that Gamper loved Barcelona – and Barcelona loved him. But he came to a tragic end in 1930 that many attribute to the climax of the anti-Spanish sentiment that's long bubbled in Catalonia. Following the restoration of the Spanish monarchy in 1923, the country found itself under the oppressive dictatorship of prime minister Miguel Primo de Rivera. During a football match against Real Madrid, Barcelona's fiercest rivals, the Catalan fans booed the Spanish anthem. As punishment for the jeering, De Rivera banned Barcelona from playing in the national league indefinitely. Meanwhile Gamper, as head of the club, was exiled to his native Switzerland and

later took his own life. Whether he did so directly as a result of being separated from Barcelona is debatable but he instantly became the club's martyr, woven into the folklore of the city.

What makes Barça a compelling vehicle for Catalan identity, and an entity that everyone from the city aristocrat to the rural farmer can associate with, is that it's owned by 180,000 members rather than a single individual or private shareholders, as most clubs are. Barcelona is the people's club. It's an image of democracy in its own right, which is in turn fuelled by the city's political history.

Since the industrialisation of Catalonia in the late 19th century, Barcelona has been a working-class city with communist, socialist and anarchic predilections. It was here in 1936, at the onset of the civil war as General Francisco Franco launched a military takeover, that the workers' revolution started. Ordinary people overthrew the inert, indecisive government to establish a republican state without hierarchy. The British writer George Orwell, who fought as a volunteer for the newly established administration, writes in *Homage to Catalonia*: "In theory it was perfect equality, and even in practice it was not far from it.... There was no one there except the peasants and ourselves, and no one owned anyone else as his master."

It was, however, a short-lived attempt at utopia. General Franco inevitably won – the people's state was too disorganised to withstand his advance – and established a 36-year regime that would suppress all Catalan identity, erase its history and outlaw its language. The dictatorship even ensured that only Real Madrid football games were aired on TV, as another form of Castilian propaganda – either you watch Madrid play or you don't watch at all.

But Barcelona football club remained one of the few places, in the crowded stands out of fascist earshot, where people could still speak Catalan and enjoy something that was their own. It was a form of escape from Franco's regime;

if Catalonia couldn't beat the oppressor in the political arena it would beat him in the sporting realm.

Since the collapse of Franco's regime in 1975, FC Barcelona has flourished. It has become one of the most successful football clubs in the world, winning the national league 14 times between 1990 and 2016. But it remains a source of civic pride and a forum of Catalan expression. So when the club's centre-back Gerard Piqué tweeted on 1 October 2017, the day of the contested Catalan independence vote, it made headline news and further rallied the city: "I've already voted. Together we're unstoppable in defending democracy."

The tweet wasn't a throwaway political comment from a celebrity. The club is as much a political entity as it is a sporting one, a dual role that has long been in the making, and it prides itself on being *més que un club*. In 2011, when discussing the idea of foreign ownership of football clubs, Barça's president Sandro Rossell stated clearly, "Barcelona is not a business, it is a feeling. Barcelona will never, ever be for sale." — (M)

Big Barça moments
—
01 1988
Manager Johan Cruyff takes over; a decade of glory follows.
02 1992
Wins its first European championship.
03 2009
Wins both domestic cups and the European championship.

ABOUT THE WRITER: Melkon Charchoglyan is a writer at MONOCLE and editor of this guide. He was delighted to return to the city where he first learned Spanish – who wouldn't want to escape a grey London for *vermut* and sunshine?

ESSAY 11
Mountain passions
Romancing on Montjuïc
—
We discover why it's practically impossible not to fall in love on Barcelona's own 'Magic Mountain'.

by Julia Keller, writer

As the saying goes, the higher you climb, the harder you fall. If applied to the laws of love, this simple reasoning would make Montjuïc, a prominent hill that rises to the southeast of Barcelona, the perfect setting in which to fall head over heels.

Whether you're hoping to woo your travel partner or make an impression on a local acquaintance, if the probability of successfully sparking the flame increases with altitude, why not give it a try? After all, Montjuïc's sweeping vistas, lush greenery and historic wealth are renowned for having sparked numerous romances among Barcelonans.

A good start for an amorous outing is to take the cable car to the top of the hill, preferably at sunset, and enjoy the spectacular views over the city from one of the various lookout points. Pack a bottle of wine, some cheese and a blanket and head to one of the hidden gardens scattered over the mountainside. Or there's always the summertime open-air cinema next to Montjuïc Castle (as the temperature drops, feign the symptoms of hypothermia and huddle closer together).

Once you've laid the romantic groundwork, it's time for things to get a little racier. You could head to Piscina Municipal de Montjuïc – arguably one of the world's most photogenic outdoor pools – and sneak into the closed-off diving area to jump from the 10-metre board while trying to look as nonchalant as the diver in Kylie Minogue's music video for "Slow", which was shot right here.

When it comes to moving on, follow Kylie's lead and take your time: the slopes of Montjuïc used to serve as Formula One racetracks until a fatal accident during the 1975 Spanish Grand Prix caused its closure. Walking is less risky anyway, so proceed uphill on foot and pay tribute to some of the city's other important sporting venues. The Olympic Stadium was originally built for the 1929 International Exposition; it was later supposed to host an anti-fascist alternative to the Berlin Olympics in 1936 but this was cancelled due to the outbreak of the Spanish Civil War, causing the stadium to fall into oblivion. More than half a century later, Barcelona hosted the 1992 Summer Olympics and the stadium had to be practically rebuilt from scratch in order to hold the games. While Monjtuïc is home to some of Barcelona's most prominent sports facilities, the Reial Club de Tennis Pompeya has managed to stay largely out of the public eye. An afternoon at this magical 1930s tennis court surrounded by pine trees can be a great way to test your partner's backhand and assess whether you're a match. Love, all.

By now you should be truly enamoured but remember to keep exploring. Head to the south side of the mountain, which is hardly visible from the city but no less enchanting than its better-known slopes. Here, perched on a cliff facing the sea and the commercial harbour, lies the vast Montjuïc Cemetery. The graveyard is closely linked to the mountain's etymology – Montjuïc comes from the Latin *Mons Judaicus*, or Mountain of the Jews, so named after a medieval Jewish graveyard. A walk through the cemetery's empty streets, past niches, tombs and pantheons, feels

> *"An afternoon at this magical tennis court surrounded by pine trees is a great way to test your partner's backhand and assess whether you're a match"*

like strolling through an alfresco sculpture museum. But the cemetery also provides a lesson in anthropology, since the hierarchy of burial spaces serves as a clear indicator of social stratification. Perhaps a little morbid for a first date but who doesn't love a bit of gothic drama?

After a marathon ascent you will reach the summit – squint a little and you may even spot the outlines of longlasting love on the horizon. From Roman times until well into the 19th century, sandstone quarried from Montjuïc was the material of choice for the most important constructions in Barcelona, and many of these buildings are still standing. May Montjuïc prove as solid a foundation for your relationship as the mountain's quarry proved for the city. — (M)

More Montjuïc
——

01 La Caseta del Migdia
Barbecue and beers in a small forest hut.
02 Palau Sant Jordi
A monumental stadium by architect Arata Isozaki.
03 Jardins de Mossèn Costa i Llobera
An impressive garden of cacti and succulents.

ABOUT THE WRITER: With her heart split between Berlin and Barcelona, Julia Keller is a writer, communications consultant and design thinker. Contrary to what you might think, she's definitely not the romantic type.

ESSAY 12
Open all hours
The tourism trap
——
Can't live with them, can't live without them. As businesses and officials scratch their heads over what to do about 'over-tourism', new hotel Casa Bonay has a few ideas.

by Inés Miró-Sans, co-founder of Casa Bonay

In recent times tourism has become one of the most hotly contested subjects in Barcelona. In 2017, major hotel openings in the city were banned, the aim being to control the enormous influx of tourists. In 2016 alone the number of visitors to pass through Barcelona hit 44 million, an 11 per cent increase on the previous year. Certainly tourism sustains a large part of our economy and many sectors of the city, from museums to public transport. But with the growing footfall come growing worries. Mass tourism – of the Times Square, stag-do variety – means prices soar, streets throng and Barcelona loses its authentic character. But rather than clamping down on tourists outright, as some suggest, surely it's a question of creating desirable tourism that livens up the city without peeving the residents.

If Casa Bonay were in charge of the city's tourism scene, what would our recipe be? Well, let's start with authenticity. Barcelona has to ensure that it's offering something that's distinctly "Barcelona", otherwise you may as well be in any other city in the world. Take food, for example. Many businesses would roll their eyes at this suggestion, since preparing food is both time-consuming and largely unprofitable, and yet cuisine is the life and soul of any establishment. Understanding a culture is as much a job for the tastebuds as any other faculty. Serve well-made fare with fresh ingredients and watch your clients purr with pleasure.

Think about what the city is missing and bring in residents. At Casa Bonay we realised that Barcelona has a million tapas bars but not a single high-quality Southeast Asian restaurant. So, alongside our local offerings we opened Elephant, Crocodile, Monkey, which has managed to attract residents in search of new culinary experiences and tourists wanting a break from *pa amb tomàquet* (bread with tomatoes). As paradoxical as this sounds, authenticity sometimes requires a small touch of the international.

Hotels – and this is where we think we know a thing or two – must stop behaving as though they're solely places to sleep. If you want to stand out and create a lasting memory, think beyond a bed for the night. You've got a sunny terrace? Good.

> "With Catalonia's resplendent natural wealth, it's a travesty not to direct visitors to the mountains, forest and sea"

Host a barbecue every month and maybe throw in the odd film screening. A sizeable ground floor? Bring in a sought-after band and invite the whole neighbourhood.

Barcelona is full of time-honoured establishments with buckets of experience and talented entrepreneurs brimming with ideas. It's a wonder we don't collaborate more. To create Casa Bonay we brought Barcelonans from every generation, from the 80-year-old mason to the 20-year-old barista. The furnishings are by a designer called Marc Morro from AOO, which is a furniture-design studio in the district of Gràcia. Nina Masó of Santa & Cole created all the lighting pieces. The tropical-themed pillows are by textile and clothing company Batabasta. And even the plants on our rooftop come courtesy of a local gardener called Alejandra Coll.

Finally, extend a way of living beyond the front lobby. From sailing getaways to grape harvests with our favourite wine producer, we've been working with our neighbours to offer our guests all sorts of adventures. And with Catalonia's resplendent natural wealth, it's a travesty not to direct the visitors to the mountains, forest and sea (beyond Platja de la Barceloneta, that is).

It's all about what Barcelona delivers and how it delivers it. The enmity towards tourism, which the media often hams up, is just scaremongering. The city welcomes all visitors with an open embrace as it has always done. And while it's down to the tourists themselves to be inquisitive, respectful and well behaved, it's up to us Barcelonans to create an environment and experience conducive to authentic, quality tourism. — (M)

Barcelona tourism
by numbers

01 Eight
Unesco World Heritage sites.
02 Twenty-six
Total Michelin stars.
03 Sixty-six
Number of museums.

ABOUT THE WRITER: A graduate of Barcelona's Esade Business School, Inés Miró-Sans is a co-founder of Casa Bonay.

Culture
—— Painting the town

A spattering of smart initiatives has seen Barcelona reclaim its place on the international art map. It's been here before: during the 19th and 20th centuries it was a hotspot for big names. As well as housing Spain's first art gallery, Sala Parés, it spawned great artists such as Miró and Antoni Tàpies while Picasso himself called the city home during his formative years. The old guard of artists can be found everywhere, from Museu Picasso in El Born to Fundació Joan Miró in Montjuïc, but you will also spy plenty of new talent promoted by plucky young gallerists who have an eagle eye on the global market.

When it comes to music, Barcelona is hard to beat. With two of Europe's best-loved music festivals and a thriving nightlife, the city is always in full swing; this is the place to come to see your favourite rock band, opera singer or flamenco guitarist. Then there are the arthouse cinemas showing a variety of films, from blockbusters to independent features in an array of languages. One thing's for certain: the culture scene here never sleeps.

Major galleries
The big picture

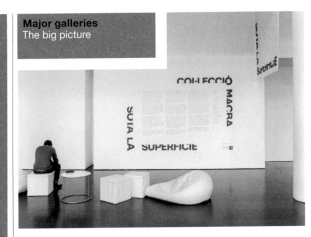

①

Macba, El Raval
Modern-art mothership

As you weave through the serpentine streets of El Raval you'll eventually hit Plaça dels Àngels, which isn't just a hotspot for Barcelona's skateboarders. It's also home to the Museu d'Art Contemporani de Barcelona (Macba), the city's main contemporary-art institution. Its permanent collection comprises about 5,000 works dating from the postwar period to the present day. There's a vast Spanish and Catalan contribution as well as international art, particularly from eastern Europe and South America.

Macba's diverse and thoughtful exhibitions have covered everything from Catalan poets to forensic architecture. All is curated under the watchful eye of director Ferran Barenblit, whose CV spans Espai 13 in Fundació Joan Miró (*see pages 97 and 118*), the New Museum in New York and Madrid's Centro de Arte Dos de Mayo.
1 Plaça dels Àngels, 08001
+34 93 412 0810
macba.cat

②
Museu Can Framis, Poblenou
Contemporary Catalan

Located in the 18th-century Can Framis textile factory, this private art collection is owned and managed by the Fundació Vila Casas, which champions contemporary Catalan art and has several galleries and museums across the region. Can Framis is devoted to modern Catalan paintings since 1960 and, with about 250 works under its roof, there's plenty to admire, including the building itself.

Many of the artists exhibited are still alive and sometimes lead talks about, and tours of, their work. Make sure you check the website to see who might be around to provide a first-hand lesson in Catalan art.

116-126 Carrer de Roc Boronat, 08018
+34 93 320 8736
fundaciovilacasas.com

③

Centre de Cultura
Contemporània de Barcelona,
El Raval
Activist art

A stone's throw from Macba
(*see page 93*) is the Centre de
Cultura Contemporània de
Barcelona (CCCB), another
mecca of contemporary art in
the city's old town. Whether it's
holding the latest immersive
show by a world-famous artist
or screening a series of films
about climate change, CCCB sits
at the forefront of Barcelona's
art scene and always has a socio-
political slant to its agenda.
Many of the events are ticketed
so it's best to book ahead.
5 Carrer de Montalegre, 08001
+ 34 93 306 4161
cccb.org

④
Museu del Disseny, Bogatell
Graphic content

Spanning graphic, fashion
and product design over four
floors, the design museum can
be explored in an afternoon.
It covers design from the 3rd
century to the present day
but the main attraction is
on the top floor. Here you'll
find a selection of works by
post-civil war poster artists
who pioneered the graphics
industry in Spain. Discover
adverts, labels and magazine
covers by names such as Josep
Artigas and his then apprentice
Josep Pla-Narbona.
37-38 Plaça de les Glòries
Catalanes, 08018
+ 34 93 256 6800
museudeldisseny.cat

⑤
CaixaForum Barcelona,
La Font de la Guatlla
Image bank

This former factory near Plaça
d'Espanya was requisitioned
by the Spanish bank La Caixa
in 1963 and became one of
the most unusual spaces in
Barcelona when it opened
as a public gallery in 2002.
It's worth visiting simply to
admire the building; be sure
to make the trip up to the roof
(*see page 116*).
    The impressive line-up
of shows that are held
within CaixaForum's walls
are an added bonus of this
architectural delight. Expect
vast exhibitions of big-name
artists, from Andy Warhol to
Giorgio de Chirico. As well as
boasting some of the most-
visited art shows in Barcelona,
each year this cultural centre
completes its programme with
talks, concerts and workshops.
6-8 Avinguda de Francesc Ferrer
i Guàrdia, 08038
+ 34 93 476 8600
caixaforum.es/barcelona/home

⑥
Museu Picasso, El Born
Pablo's palace

Though Pablo Picasso was born in Málaga and spent much of his life in France, Barcelona was the place he called home and where he honed his talents early on. Much of the art here was donated by Picasso himself, as well as his friends and other artists such as Salvador Dalí. Paintings, lithographs, sketches and ceramics are hung across five adjoining gothic townhouses.

This collection showcases the wealth of styles and formats that the artist developed during his lifetime. It's also the only place in the world with a complete series of works, namely his "Las Meninas": a 58-piece interpretation of Diego Velázquez's painting of the same name.
15-23 Carrer Montcada, 08003
+34 93 256 3000
museupicasso.bcn.cat

Catalan art
Frames of reference

1

Fundació Joan Miró, Montjuïc
Modern art at its peak

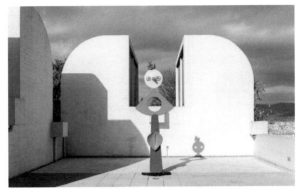

Situated at the top of Montjuïc,
just behind the Palau Nacional,
this gallery is home to works by
the Barcelonan surrealist artist
Joan Miró. Here Miró's vivid
colours pop against the white
concrete walls of a fantastical
modernist structure by Josep
Lluís Sert. The foundation
was set up by the artist himself,
along with friend and local
gallerist Joan Prats (*see page
101*), to share the collection
and promote the research of
contemporary art.

Soon after opening in 1975,
Espai 13 was also established.
This smaller space within
the gallery exhibits works by
contemporary artists that
complement Miró's oeuvre,
as well as guest works by the
likes of Alexander Calder.
Parc de Montjuïc, 08038
+ 34 93 443 9470
fmirobcn.org

②
Mnac, Montjuïc
A thorough education

The Palau Nacional is an
impressive opus of 20th-
century Spanish architecture
perched at the foot of Montjuïc.
Since 1934 it's also been the
home of the Museu Nacional
d'Art de Catalunya (Mnac).

Start here if you want to get
to grips with Catalan art before
you visit Barcelona's more
contemporary-focused galleries
– Mnac will take you back
much further. The collection
showcases a comprehensive,
chronological guide – from
medieval to modern – to the
many artists and designers that
Catalonia has produced over
the centuries. Between May
and October, nip up to the roof
for a stunning view of the city.
*Palau Nacional, Parc de
Montjuïc, 08038
+34 93 622 0360
museunacional.cat*

③

Fundació Suñol,
Dreta de l'Eixample
Small but perfectly formed

Fundació Suñol is a small, unassuming haven of art among the busy shopping streets of Passeig de Gràcia. Spread across three floors and a courtyard, it exhibits the collection of Barcelona's Josep Suñol, one of Spain's foremost art collectors of the 20th century.

Suñol was a great friend of Fernando Vijande, a catalytic character in the world of Spanish art during the 1960s, especially when it came to the avant garde. The friendship put Suñol in the thick of an exciting new art scene, allowing him to amass a catalogue of more than 1,200 works. The majority of his collection is by Catalan artists but you'll also find works by renowned names from around the world.
98 Passeig de Gràcia, 08008
+34 93 496 1032
fundaciosunol.org

①

Sala Parés, Barri Gòtic
Old master

Sala Parés is the oldest art gallery in Spain. It started out as an art supplies shop owned by Joan Parés, who in 1877 decided to begin showing what his customers were creating. By 1884 the building had been extended and was showing the most prominent Catalan artists of the day, including Ramón Casas.

By 1925 the Parés family had closed shop and the Maragall family had taken over. "Sala Parés was the first place to exhibit Picasso in Barcelona," says Helena, the daughter of current owner Joan Anton Maragall. The family also runs Galeria Trama upstairs, which focuses on contemporary art.
5 Carrer Petritxol, 08002
+34 93 318 7020
salapares.com

②
Galeria Senda, El Born
Heart of the art scene

Located in the district recently dubbed "TrafalgArt" (it makes sense when you see the street name), Senda is one of several institutions turning this area into Barcelona's new art hub. The gallery is spread across three levels, designed by local architect Carles Puig and interior designer Maria Antònia Mir. You might catch wooden sculptures by German artist Stephan Balkenhol or paintings by Nobel Prize-winning writer Gao Xingjian.
32 Carrer de Trafalgar, 08010
+34 93 487 6759
galeriasenda.com

③
ADN Galeria, L'Antiga Esquerra de l'Eixample
What a performance

"Our programme has a clear focus on the links between art, society and politics," says founder Miguel Ángel Sánchez, who opened this gallery in 2003. Whether they're by Catalans such as Jordi Colomer or international artists, including Moroccan-French Bouchra Khalili, the pieces at ADN pack a punch.

There's also installation and performance art, as well as a further two spaces on the edge of the city. ADN Platform explores the relationship between art and society and ADN Factory is a base for artists to develop their installations.
49 Carrer d'Enric Granados, 08008
+34 93 451 0064
adngaleria.com

⑤
ProjecteSD, Dreta de
l'Eixample
Private viewing

Ask anyone who works within
Barcelona's art scene for a list
of their favourite galleries and
ProjecteSD will likely come up.
Situated on a neat avenue of
galleries, it's less conspicuous
than its neighbours.

Head through the wrought-
iron doors and down a corridor
to explore this well-curated
compact space. You'll find
works that unite established
artists and younger creatives,
including Mexican artist
Iñaki Bonillas and Barcelonan
Patrícia Dauder.
8 Passatge de Mercader, 08008
+34 93 488 1360
projectesd.com

④
Galeria Joan Prats,
Dreta de l'Eixample
Friends in high places

Joan Prats was a revered
promoter of art in the 20th
century and a close friend
of Joan Miró. The duo had
known each other since art
school and together founded
the Fundació Joan Miró (*see
pages 97 and 118*).

Galeria Joan Prats opened
in 1976, six years after Prats
died, and continues to promote
contemporary artists. It's
located just off Carrer del
Consell de Cent in Eixample,
one of the original hubs for
art galleries in Barcelona.
54 Carrer de Balmes, 08007
+34 93 216 0284
galeriajoanprats.com

⑥
Side Gallery, L'Antiga
Esquerra de l'Eixample
Latin classics

The small Side Gallery
concentrates on mid-20th
century to contemporary names
who straddle the worlds of art
and design. There's a focus on
Latin American and Spanish
designers: big 20th-century
players such as architect
Oscar Niemeyer, furniture
designer Joaquim Tenreiro and
interior designer Clara Porset.
You'll also find present-day
artists from elsewhere, such as
London-based lighting maestro
Michael Anastassiades.
*80 Carrer d'Enric Granados,
08008*
+34 93 162 1575
side-gallery.com

Live venues
Sounds of the city

①
Palau de la Música Catalana,
El Born
Pulling out all the stops

Designed in the early 20th
century for the choral society
Orfeó Català by *modernisme*
heavyweight Lluís Domènech
i Montaner, the city's music
hall is an incredible feat of
grandeur that was awarded
Unesco World Heritage status
in 1997. The interiors are
awash with intricate flowers,
flags and mythological figures.
At the back of the stage is
an impressive organ, while
perhaps the most striking
part of the hall is the bulbous
stained-glass skylight.
 If you can't make it to a
concert it's worth signing up
for one of the half-hourly tours,
and be sure to check out the
balcony above the stage. Part
of the former apartment of
Lluís Millet i Pagès, co-founder
of the choir, it puts any home
cinema to shame.
4-6 Carrer Palau de la Música,
08003
+34 93 295 7200
palaumusica.cat

We'll soon be
on stage!

❷
Sala Apolo, Poble-sec
Music of the gods

Sala Apolo's programme will make music-lovers weep with joy, featuring both big acts and local talent spanning rock, pop, ska, jazz, electro and more. It looks like an old theatre with high ceilings and red-velvet mezzanines but don't let that regalia fool you: this is *the* place for a party. After gigs the club nights here are perennially popular, as are those in sister venue La [2] de Apolo, which is a little smaller but has a great sound system.
113 Carrer Nou de la Rambla, 08004
+34 93 441 4001
sala-apolo.com

③
JazzSí Club, El Raval
Up close and personal

This small concert hall may be hard to find but it's well worth seeking out. It has a daily programme of gigs that celebrates young jazz and flamenco musicians in particular. With close ties to the local Taller de Músics music school, JazzSí has a constant rotation of local talent on stage. It is a great spot for a glass of wine and an intimate performance, and to get to grips with the music of Spain and other traditions. Get here early to grab a seat.
2 Carrer de Requesens, 08001
+34 93 329 0020
tallerdemusics.com/jazzsi-club

Best of the 'festes'

01 **Primavera Sound, El Besòs i el Maresme:** Perhaps Barcelona's most famous festival, Primavera (*see page 83*) is the hot ticket every May/June. It boasts more than a dozen stages that welcome some of the best international bands and DJs, alongside lots of homegrown talent.
primaverasound.com

02 **Sónar Festival, various locations:** Since 1994, big names have graced the stages of Sónar, which now takes place in the Fira Gran Via de l'Hospitalet convention centre on the outskirts of the city. It also runs Sónar+D, a daytime conference on music and technology, which takes place elsewhere.
sonar.es

03 **Festa Major de Gràcia, Gràcia:** This week-long event in August is one of the city's most renowned traditional festivals (*see page 79*). Every *carrer* (street) is decked out under a different theme, turning Gràcia into a colourful euphony of street parties.
festamajordegracia.cat

Join the circle

Catalonia's traditional dance, the *sardana*, may not have the drama of flamenco but it's a much more sociable affair, performed by a group of people in a circle and accompanied by a woodwind band called a *cobla*. Look out for alfresco performances in the *places* of Barri Gòtic.

Cinema
Screen scene

01 Barcelona, 1994: In this romantic comedy set in the 1980s, Whit Stillman explores the culture clash between the US and Barcelona.

02 Todo sobre mi madre (All About My Mother), 1999: Expect shots of the city's greatest monuments in the film that's often hailed as the best of Pedro Almodóvar's career.

03 L'Auberge Espagnole (The Spanish Apartment), 2002: A coming-of-age comedy about French Erasmus student Xavier (Romain Duris), who opts for a year in Barcelona over a tedious job in Paris.

04 Vicky Cristina Barcelona, 2008: Rebecca Hall, Javier Bardem and Scarlett Johansson get tangled up in a love triangle in Woody Allen's film, which paints a picture-perfect vision of Barcelona.

05 Biutiful, 2010 Javier Bardem received an Oscar nomination for his portrayal of Uxbal, a single father trying to escape the darker fringes of the city in Alejandro González Iñárritu's drama.

①

Cines Verdi, Gràcia
Talking your language

A common gripe about seeing English-language films in non-English-speaking countries is that they are often dubbed rather than subtitled. One cinema in Barcelona that's bucking the trend and offering a mixture of international arthouse and mainstream films in the original tongue (with either English or Catalan subtitles) is Cines Verdi.

Located in the leafy neighbourhood of Gràcia, Cines Verdi offers a relaxing dose of culture and a welcome break from the local boutiques. The nine screens are fairly small but the tickets are reasonably priced. One thing to note is that the cinema is split across two streets: Cines Verdi is on Carrer de Verdi and Verdi Park is directly behind on Carrer de Torrijos. Check you have the right address for your screen.
32 Carrer de Verdi, 08012
+34 93 238 7990
cines-verdi.com

②

Zumzeig, Hostafrancs
Films for thought

In late 2016 this non-profit cinema underwent a head-to-toe makeover and the results have made it a trailblazer for arthouse cinemas in the city. Run by a co-operative dedicated to screenings that will spark conversation and unite the local community, the smart 73-seat auditorium shows films that are picked from an eclectic roster of international and independent features, shorts, documentaries and art features. Adjoining the screen is a small French-inspired bistro with a well-stocked bar.
53 Carrer de Béjar, 08014
+34 93 546 1411
zumzeigcine.coop

Movie mountain

If you're planning a summer trip to the city then check out the line-up at Sala Montjuïc, Barcelona's outdoor cinema at Montjuïc Castle. Enjoy some of the biggest films of the year while taking in fantastic views of Barcelona's skyline.
salamontjuic.org

Media round-up
Talking points

① Media
Page-turners

Catalan-language press is thriving. ❶ *El Punt Avui* and ❷ *Ara* are two broadsheets launched in the past decade, while ❸ *La Vanguardia*, Catalonia's reputed news title, has been printing since 1881 and in Catalan since 2011.

Niche-interest magazines also abound. Gardeners ought to flick through English-language ❹ *The Plant*, which covers all things flora. ❺ *Perdiz*, founded by Marta Puigdemasa, writes biannually on all things related to happiness in both English and Spanish.

Spanish language ❻ *El Ciervo* and Catalan ❼ *L'Avenç* – the former published every two months, the latter monthly – offer a profound academic voice on history, culture and current affairs. For a less scholastic tone on culture and design there are biannual

Spanish-language ❽ *Ajoblanco*, Catalan ❾ *Núvol* (it launched its first print issue in 2017) and literary review ❿ *Quimera*, published monthly.

Interior design and architecture titles ⓫ *Openhouse* and ⓬ *Apartamento* peek into the most fascinating spaces around the world, both in English. ⓭ *Altaïr* offers long-form essays on travel and culture, while ⓮ *Volata* is the go-to for cycling aficionados.

Don't mind me, just catching up on some reading

Radio round-up

01 Catalunya Ràdio: Catalonia's public broadcaster. Seasoned journalist Mònica Terribas leads the weekday morning show, *El matí de Catalunya Ràdio*.
ccma.cat/catradio

02 RAC1: The top-rated Catalan-language station.
rac1.cat

03 Ràdio Web Macba: An internet station run by the Museu d'Art Contemporani de Barcelona.
rwm.macba.cat

04 Radio Gladys Palmera: Mixes by top Latin American DJs.
gladyspalmera.com

05 Barcelona City FM: Barcelona's only English-speaking radio station.
barcelonacityfm.com

Design and architecture
—— The built environment

Few cities in the world are as architecturally rich as Barcelona. The beguiling fairytale structures of Antoni Gaudí and his *modernistes* contemporaries defined the city's visual identity and have inspired more than a century of imaginative, and at times surreal, architecture.

But this is also a city that has refused to rest on its laurels. Look no further than the 1992 Olympics for proof: the Catalan capital reinvented itself with an explosion of cutting-edge creations, celebrating the games with innovative structures and a trailblazing tradition of both graphic and industrial design.

So while we explore the marvels of *modernisme* we also delve deep into Barcelona's architectural landscape, unlocking its lesser-known gems. There are modernist masterpieces that defied the monotony of the fascist period, sci-fi-style social housing projects and residential curios dotting the Eixample neighbourhood, not to mention the awe-inspiring skyscrapers and contemporary wonders on the city's skyline.

Modernisme
Urban fairytales

①
Casa Comalat, Dreta de l'Eixample
Double the appeal

Architect Salvador Valeri i Pupurull's 1911 creation sits on a triangular plot of land that affords it two different façades. The main view on Avinguda Diagonal is symmetrical and majestic, with a romantic flourish: the banisters on the balconies resemble the grille on a knight's helmet and echo Gaudí's nearby Casa Batlló, the epitome of *modernisme*.

The side facing Carrer de Còrsega is more magical: colourful, irregular bay windows curve around like a colourful tree and the ceramic glaze patterning that adorns the full façade further underlines Pupurull's unique style. Sadly the building isn't open to the public but there's more than enough to admire outside.
442 Avinguda Diagonal, 08037

②

Recinte Modernista de Sant
Pau, Guinardó
Healing environment

This 27-pavilion complex
suffers from sitting behind La
Sagrada Família (*see page 111*),
which inevitably steals some
of its thunder. But this work of
modernisme is not to be missed.

The former hospital was
designed by Lluís Domènech
i Montaner, who died seven
years before it was finished in
1930. He believed in the healing
nature of beauty so he decked
the grounds with stained glass,
ornate façades, allegorical
statues and all the other proper
touches of *modernisme*. Indeed,
if Gaudí's works celebrate
the style, this is its carnival. It
was awarded Unesco World
Heritage status in 1997.
*167 Carrer de Sant Antoni
Maria Claret, 08025
+34 93 553 7801
santpaubarcelona.org*

③

Casa de les Punxes, Dreta de l'Eixample
Dragon layered

This fanciful house by *modernista* architect Josep Puig i Cadafalch embodies the story of Sant Jordi (Saint George), Catalonia's patron saint. Cadafalch's main influence was Neuschwanstein Castle in Bavaria, as seen in the casa's soaring, conical spires.

On the roof are four plaques: three pay homage to the sisters of the Terradas family, for whom the house was built, and one depicts Sant Jordi, invoking him to guard the building. It's a place steeped in allegory and fairytale romance – even the bright shingles on the roof resemble the reddish-green scales of the dragon that the saint vanquished.
420 Avinguda Diagonal, 08036
+ 34 93 016 0128
casadelespunxes.es

④

Casa Amatller, Dreta de l'Eixample
Fusion of styles

As the ziggurat-style roofing of the building suggests, architect Josep Puig i Cadafalch drew on a breadth of architectural sources to design this house for chocolate magnate Antoni Amatller, from neo-gothic to golden-age Amsterdam.

The interior is an explosion of *modernisme*. With twisting pink-marble columns, romanesque mosaic floors and ornate carriage-sized fireplaces, Casa Amatller makes as great an impression today as it did when completed in 1900.
41 Passeig de Gràcia, 08007
+ 34 93 461 7460
amatller.org

Modernisme

Modernisme is often referred to as Catalan art nouveau but such a proxy epithet doesn't do the style justice. All eight of Barcelona's World Heritage Unesco-listed buildings are products of the movement.

Modernisme was born in the 1870s when Barcelona was enjoying industrial prosperity and had recently expanded beyond its medieval walls. This afforded architects such as Antoni Gaudí and Josep Puig i Cadafalch a torrent of commissions and new neighbourhoods in which to erect the structures of their dreams. This historic period of flourishes was known as the *renaixença* (renaissance) and brought with it a resurgence of Catalan identity, which *modernisme* sought to manifest in architectural form.

In homage to Catalan history, gothic, Moorish and medieval styles were woven together with the nature-inspired motifs of art nouveau; allegorical themes found expression on splendid façades; and imaginative, colourful materials such as *trencadís* (broken ceramic tiles) took centre stage. The buildings that this period produced are fairytales told with bricks and mortar rather than ink and paper.

Although the movement dwindled and finally fizzled out in 1911, it made an undeniable impression on the look of the city and continues to inspire architects in the modern era.

Early 20th century
Post modernisme

① BBVA Bank, Barri Gòtic
Conspicuous wealth

A muscular structure that
screams prosperity and
modernity – or it did in 1939,
when Barcelona was booming
– this art deco building by
architect José Yárnoz Larrosa
and painter Luis Menéndez
Pidal seems more fitting for
Wall Street than Barcelona.
Once the regional HQ of the
Bank of Spain, today it houses
the offices of BBVA bank. Left
and right of the entrance are
two statues, one holding the
cog of industry and the other
the crest of Catalonia: an
unambiguous statement of
the building's purpose.
6 Plaça d'Antoni Maura, 08003

② Barcelona Pavilion, Montjuïc
Reconstructed glory

Also known as the German
Pavilion, this gem was designed
by Mies van der Rohe for the
1929 Barcelona International
Exposition. Through green
marble, travertine, onyx, steel
and glass he manifests the
rebirth, modernity and honesty
that Germany sought to express
after the First World War.
While the furniture (including
the white-leather Barcelona
chair) is original, the structure
is a reconstruction. It was
dismantled after the exposition
but rebuilt in the 1980s by
Catalan architects.
*7 Avinguda de Francesc Ferrer
i Guàrdia, 08038
+34 93 215 1011
miesbcn.com*

③ Casa Xina, L'Antiga Esquerra
de l'Eixample
Fine China

When Valencian architect Joan
Guardiola unveiled Casa Xina
in 1930, writer Manuel Brunet
labelled it "a new milestone
for the museum of horrors",
a ridiculous offshoot of the
numerous *modernista* buildings
that had been similarly derided
two decades earlier.
   As with *modernisme*, time
has mollified the city's opinion
of Guardiola's eccentricity. Art
deco-inspired motifs abound,
with pagoda fans on the upper
ledge and Egyptian-revivalist
graffito medallions dotting the
façade. The interior is equally
wondrous but you'll need to
befriend a resident to see it.
54 Carrer de Muntaner, 08011

Gaudí
Design pioneer

01 02

06 07

08 09   10

03

04 05

11

12

Antoni Gaudí i Cornet (1852 to 1926) altered Barcelona's visual identity immeasurably. Inspired by neo-gothic and oriental styles, and drawing on natural shapes and imagery, he drove the *modernisme* movement and left a distinct mark on the city's urban look.

01 — 02 La Sagrada Família, Sagrada Família: Under construction from Gaudí's blueprints since 1882; completion is slated for 2026.
sagradafamilia.org

03 — 05 Casa Vicens, Gràcia: The first of Gaudí's major casas, finished in 1885. Its style fuses an array of architectural traditions such as Moorish-revival.
casavicens.org

06 Palau Güell, Barri Gòtic: Designed for Gaudí's patron, Eusebi Güell, this house is more neo-gothic. Its wrought-iron façade is a wonder.
palauguell.cat

07 Casa Milà, Dreta de l'Eixample: Also known as La Pedrera (The Stone Quarry). Its chimneys resemble veiled faces, perhaps a nod to Spain's Islamic heritage.
lapedrera.com

08 Torre Bellesguard, Sarrià-Sant Gervasi: Emulates the 15th-century castle of Martin I, King of Aragón, on the site of which it's built.
bellesguardgaudi.com

09 — 10 Parc Güell, Gràcia: Head here for a taste of Gaudí's eccentric gingerbread-like houses.
parkguell.cat

11 — 12 Casa Batlló, Dreta de l'Eixample: This house resembles a cross-section of a dragon: the tiled roof is the scaly skin and the skeletal balconies the creatures it has consumed.
casabatllo.es

Residential
Living spaces

❶
La Ricarda, El Prat
de Llobregat
Smart home

For decades La Ricarda was a haven for Barcelona's intelligentsia, from Joan Miró to Josep Lluís Sert. Catalan architect Antoni Bonet designed the modernist masterpiece as a country house for close friend Ricardo Gomis in 1963; the planning and construction took more than a decade, with Bonet scrapping an initial design in favour of the current style.

Gomis' daughter Marita describes the house as "an undulating roof floating in the air", in reference to the series of concrete-roofed pavilions that make up the complex. Bonet even designed a collection of avant garde furniture to suit the home, pairing his pieces with finds from Japan and Scandinavia, such as Hans J Wegner chairs. Call ahead to arrange a visit.
Finca La Ricarda, 08820
+34 93 212 4582

(2)
Walden 7, Sant Just Desvern
Futuristic feel

To conceive this utopian social-housing project, architect Ricardo Bofill decamped to the Algerian desert in the 1970s with a handful of poets, philosophers and sociologists in search of an architectural vision. The result is Walden 7, whose name comes from the 1948 sci-fi novel *Walden Two*.

Inside the terracotta-hued social-housing complex are 446 apartments, as well as gardens, fountains and two rooftop swimming pools (complete with a nudist section). The structure is also modular: the ceramic-tiled walls can be manipulated to add an extra window or join two apartments together for more space. It's a grand utopian experiment that, since 1975, has drawn as many intellectuals enamoured by Walden 7's idealist design as working-class families wanting better living standards.
106 Carretera Reial, 08960
+ 34 93 371 8063
walden7.com

③

Casa Bloc, Sant Andreu
Improved housing

In the early 20th century, Barcelona's central *barris* were often cramped and ill suited to modern standards of living. Casa Bloc was an early attempt at intelligent social housing, built in 1939 by a group of Catalan architects (Josep Lluís Sert among them) and inspired by the European bauhaus movement.

The "two-shape" design meant that all apartments faced east or southeast for maximum sunlight. Living quarters were laid out to accommodate modern amenities – such as a separate toilet, shower and kitchen – and the balcony doors could be folded to extend the living room onto the terrace.
*95-101 Passeig de Torras
i Bages, 08030*
+34 93 256 6800
museudeldisseny.cat

Contemporary
New and exciting

①

Ciutat de la Justícia,
L'Hospitalet de Llobregat
The law in order

The palaces of justice used to be scattered across Barcelona in 17 different buildings. To make the system more efficient, the city brought the entire department together near the *barri* of La Bordeta – and invited David Chipperfield to add a splash of elegance and colour to the results.

Erected in 2009, the complex comprises eight lattice-like buildings. Thanks to the varying soft palettes there's something of a cheerful Lego-block feel about them, albeit mixed with the menacing austerity of uniform appearance appropriate to the courts of law. The buildings are best viewed from a distance; if you do get up close to them, we hope it's of your own accord.
*111 Gran Via de les Corts
Catalanes, 08075*
+34 93 554 8600
ciutatdelajusticia.com

②

Diagonal ZeroZero, El Besòs
i el Maresme
Shining example

With its distinctive futuristic appearance, this skyscraper by architecture firm EMBA was constructed in just over three years and completed in 2011. It's a structure seemingly tense with energy, a trapezoidal prism covered in an irregular diamond lattice whose edges protrude beyond the surface of the glass. Late-night revellers returning from Primavera Sound (*see page 83*) at Parc del Fòrum should steal a look in its direction: the building is even more of a sight to behold when illuminated.
*5 Plaça d'Ernest Lluch
i Martin, 08019*

Repurposed
New uses for old buildings

③
Porta Fira Towers, L'Hospitalet de Llobregat
Sibling structures

These two towers – completed in 2010 by Japanese architect Toyo Ito and Barcelona studio b720 Fermín Vázquez Arquitectos – are an inevitable sight en route to the airport. One is the twisting, mushroom-like Hotel Porta Fira, its furrowed exterior a sea of red-aluminium rods fastened by ball-joints, giving the building a shimmering form. Its neighbour, the Torre Realia BCN office building, may seem sombre and proud by comparison but note the red "H" writhing down its centre, echoing the hotel's organic form and creating a dialogue between the structures.
45 Plaça d'Europa, 08908
+34 93 297 3500 (Hotel Porta Fira)
hotelbarcelonaportafira.com

①
Las Arenas, La Nova Esquerra de l'Eixample
No-bull enterprise

The city is divided over the aesthetic value of this former bullring but everyone agrees on its symbolic importance. Catalonia officially banned bullfighting in 2010 but Las Arenas hadn't held a fight since 1977, with the practice long in decline. Rather than demolish the impressive fin-de-siècle stadium – a gem of the Moorish-revival style – architects Richard Rogers and Alonso y Balaguer repurposed it in 2011 to create a shopping centre and symbol of how the city has moved on.
   The duo replaced the plinth that once underpinned the structure with a reinforced concrete-and-metal footing, necessary to support the added mass of shops and restaurants. At the top of the ring is a 300-metre-long viewing promenade circling a 76-metre-wide dome, one of the largest in Europe.
373-385 Gran Via de les Corts Catalanes, 08015
+34 93 289 0244
arenasdebarcelona.com

If you ask me it's all about Miró

②
Dipòsit de les Aigües,
Vila Olímpica
Trickle-down learning

The structure next to Parc de
la Ciutadella has served many
purposes since its completion
in 1876, homeless shelter,
police garage and justice
archive among them. But it was
designed as a reservoir for the
park's fountains.

Architect Josep Fontserè,
aided by a young Gaudí,
mimicked Roman designs and
hollowed the interior with tall
arches to reduce materials
without affecting the structure.
Now the Dipòsit regulates
the flow of knowledge instead
of water: in 1999 architects
Lluís Clotet and Ignacio
Paricio repurposed it into the
Universitat Pompeu Fabra's
central library. Take a tour.
25-27 Ramon Trias Fargas, 08005
+34 93 542 2000
upf.edu

③
CaixaForum Barcelona,
La Font de la Guatlla
Factory fresh

On its completion in 1911,
Josep Puig i Cadafalch's
textile factory married an
imaginative style that took its
cue from medieval castles with
the latest standards of modern
construction. Unlike other
exports of *modernisme*, the
building received instant praise
at a time when Barcelona was
expanding and industrialising.

The factory stood empty
for decades before serving
as a police station for 50
years. Then, in 2002, it gained
a new lease on life as a
cultural centre. Owner
La Caixa invited Japanese
architect Arata Isozaki to
oversee its transformation.
While respecting the original
structure he added modern
flourishes, such as a steel-and-
glass awning over the entrance.
6-8 Avinguda de Francesc Ferrer
i Guàrdia, 08038
+34 93 476 8600
caixaforum.es

Surreal
Weird and wonderful

①
La Fábrica, Sant Just Desvern
Post industrial

In 1973 the sound of dynamite
echoed through the district of
Sant Just as architect Ricardo
Bofill transformed a former
cement factory into his home
and office. Although sections
of the monstrous structure
were torn down – you can
still see the marks of the old
perimeter from the roof of
Walden 7 next door (*see page
113*) – the architect preserved
the factory's central complex
and industrial essence.

The jungle of trees and the
long, gothic-style windows are
the few additions made by Bofill
to the six former silos. The rest
is an homage to the building's
past, most noticeable in La
Catedral, the central conference
room. It's so called after its
nave-like property, where the
conical tips of cement mixers
hang over parquet floors and
architectural maquettes.
*14 Avenida de la Indústria,
08960*
+34 93 499 9900
ricardobofill.com

**Casa de
Xavier Corberó**
—
Late sculptor Xavier Corberó
left behind a labyrinthine
house of concrete arches
stacked upon concrete arches,
resembling a Giorgio de Chirico
painting. Though it's open only
on special occasions you can
sneak a glimpse over the gates.
Carrer Montserrat, 08950

117

❷

Fundació Joan Miró, Montjuïc
Head in the clouds

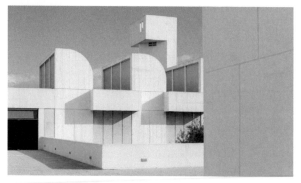

Despite the apparent irregularity of Josep Lluís Sert's 1975 modernist masterpiece, which seemingly rolls away to infinity like a chain of clouds, the Catalan architect applied a great deal of structure and foresight to the building's design in order to facilitate how people engage with the art on display there.

Sert organised the purpose-built complex around a central courtyard, towards which the movement of visitors spirals, meaning that you never pass the same room twice. The spiral design also affords the use of ramps, so that art-lovers may enter the galleries from above and circle down to Miró's gigantic works, thus appreciating them from all angles.

Parc de Montjuïc, 08038
+ 34 93 443 9470
fmirobcn.org

③

Parc de l'Espanya Industrial, Sants
Water feature

This little park, reminiscent of De Chirico's "I Bagni Misteriosi", occupies the site of the former La España Industrial textile mill, which was turned into a park after its closure in the 1970s. Though sources suggest he was inspired by ancient Roman baths, Basque architect Luis Peña Ganchegui must have been dreaming of a Dalí painting when drafting the designs.

Nine lighthouse-like turrets crown the steps that descend past cypresses to a small artificial lake. Next to it is Andrés Nagel's vast, abstract "El Drac", a statue of a dragon that also serves as a children's slide – a popular attraction with the little ones despite its terrifying appearance.

37 Carrer de Muntadas, 08014

Olympics
Gold-medal structures

①

Viviendas Olímpicas, Vila Olímpica
Athletes' village

The most noteworthy thing about Ricardo Bofill's Olympic apartments, designed to house the athletes of the 1992 games, is the foresight of the design. Unlike most Olympic complexes, which dazzle the eye but seem ridiculous after the events conclude, the 113 terracotta-hued apartments have remained in harmony with their surroundings more than 25 years later.

Bofill went with ziggurat-style steps throughout the design, affording the inhabitants of the main tower greater privacy; for the apartments in the buildings below, they meant sun-filled terraces. A recurring theme in Bofill's residential buildings, space was reserved for private gardens on the interior side of the ground floor, while the side overlooking the street features shops and communal spaces.
Corner of Carrer del Doctor Trueta and Carrer de l'Arquitecte Sert

②

Peix Olímpic, Barceloneta
Maritime imagery

In the run up to the 1992 Olympics, Barcelona was blooming with design and architecture projects. Perhaps the most iconic, Frank Gehry's "Olympic Fish" sculpture, swum its way into the city's visual identity immediately – and has been a much loved fixture in Barcelona ever since.

The US-based architect used layers of intertwining gilded steel to create the scaly skeleton, shaped into a kink as though the giant fish is about to leap into the sea. It can also be said to resemble the hull of a ship: an appropriate image for a city of seafarers, especially with the Monument a Cristòfor Colom just along the road.
2 Carrer de Ramon Trias Fargas, 08005

③

Torre de Comunicacions de Montjuïc, Montjuïc
Variations on a theme

This 136-metre steel structure shoots into the sky, much like an Olympic torch. The functioning telecommunications tower also acts as a sundial – you'll see its gargantuan shadow creeping across the Plaça d'Espanya.

It's a tower packed with competing imagery. Valencian architect Santiago Calatrava conceived its image as an athlete kneeling to receive a medal. And the pedestal that receives the genuflecting figure? A waving crescent base of *trencadís* (shattered ceramic tiles): a nod to Gaudí, who popularised the material.
Carrer Pierre de Coubertin, 08038

Wild card

Edgy designer Javier Mariscal is known for his loud, colourful style, which he applied to everything from film animation to eccentric, bulbous furniture. What really won him worldwide fame, however, was Cobi, the mascot of the 1992 Barcelona Olympics (*see page 76*).
mariscal.com

Markets
Stall stories

①
Mercat dels Encants, Fort Pienc
Market with a twist

This flea market dates back to the 13th century but its new home, finished in 2013 by b720 Fermín Vázquez Arquitectos, is grand and unique. In fact, it's hardly a building at all, more a spiralling stairway packed with market stalls (as well as the odd bar) and crowned by a splintered awning whose underside is made of stainless steel. You'll note the general absence of walls: a wise decision from the architects for the design of such a crowded and raucous public space.
158 Carrer de los Castillejos, 08013
+34 93 245 2299
encantsbcn.com

②
Mercat de Santa Caterina, El Born
Historic location

With a site that included a Roman burial ground and a 13th-century church in the historic centre, architects EMBT had their work cut out when they were commissioned to replace the old market in 1997. Fortunately, what they unveiled in 2005 won the approval of all.

The 100 stalls are covered by 325,000 colourful ceramic tiles in an undulating roof, the latter's panels so complex they had to be cut by hand. Viewed from above it resembles a polychrome tortoise.
16 Avinguda de Francesc Cambó, 08003
+34 93 319 5740

③
Mercabarna-flor, Sant Boi de Llobregat
Flower powered

Willy Müller Architects' gigantic flower market is a multi-colour flash of lightning designed to resemble rows of flowers in bloom. But it's not all just slick veneer: a series of solar panels along the angled roof powers three distinct climates within the building.

The first section maintains crisp temperatures between 2C and 15C for flowers with a quick turnover, while species with greater longevity are kept between 15C and 26C. The central section, for dried flowers, is designed for close monitoring and extinguishing fires – sensible, given the old market burned down in 2001.
1 Carretera Antiga de València, 08830
+34 93 556 8310
mercabarnaflor.com

01

02

03

04

05　06

07

08　09

01 The Eixample grid: In 1854 Barcelona tore down its medieval walls to expand the city boundaries. Development of new neighbourhood Eixample (literally "expansion") fell to urban-planner Ildefons Cerdà. He designed some 500 octagonal blocks, 16 metres in height and facing northwest or southeast for maximum light. He intended only two sides of each block to be built up, with the space between reserved for parks. Sadly the blocks grew far beyond that, the open sides built up in later years.

02 — 03 Paving stones: Each district in Barcelona has a unique *panot* (paving stone), designed by an eminent architect. The classic is Eixample's Flor de Barcelona, a four-leaf flower by Josep Puig i Cadafalch. Passeig de Gràcia has Gaudí's hexagonal creation, while on Avinguda Diagonal it's a banana leaf designed in 2014 by Terradas Arquitectos.

04 — 07 Street sculptures: In the run up to the 1992 Olympics a swathe of public artwork was commissioned to brighten the streets. Some are quirky and fun (Javier Mariscal's giant prawn statue "Gambrinus"), while others, particularly Rebecca Horn's "L'Estel ferit" ("Wounded Star", a stack of four steel blocks on Platja de la Barceloneta), are melancholy works that touch on Barcelona's past while signalling its future.

08 — 09 Modernista doorways: During the boom of *modernisme*, a building's entrance was a way to display skill (in the artist's case) and wealth (in the patron's). Stained glass, allegorical engravings, ceramic tiling and floral ornaments: no two are the same in shape or adornment.

Sport and fitness
—— We can work it out

In a city as sun-drenched as this, you don't want to be holed up in museums and shops all day long. Barcelona is overrun with outdoor opportunities – no, we're not just talking about a rooftop *vermut* – and our selection has been put together with a sense of discovery in mind.

Ever since the transformative 1992 Summer Olympic Games, the Catalan capital has pushed on with urban renewal. It's been reimagining its coastline, waterways and upper hills – and creating fertile ground for fitness buffs in the process. The exercise epicentre is around Barceloneta but we recommend heading into the hills of Montjuïc and the Serra de Collserola national park to avoid the crowds.

As far as beaches go, we've included a handful of less-besieged swimming spots on the city's fringes, as well as gyms, pools, a surf school and a bouldering centre for good measure. You'll also find some specially chosen sanctums for attaining inner peace to accompany that bronzed body.

①
Club Natació Barcelona, Barceloneta
Aquatic excellence

When this pool opened as CNB Banys Orientals in 1907 its 20 founding members paid a paltry fee of just two pesetas to enjoy it. Today the vast facility includes two outdoor pools (one salt water, the other heated) and two indoor pools, as well as beach-volleyball courts, a martial-arts studio and gym.

And this club is serious about the pursuit of sporting excellence: it has trained more than 166 Olympians and hundreds of swimmers, water-polo players and triathletes.
93 Passeig de Joan de Borbó, 08039
+34 93 221 4600
cnb.cat

②

Piscina Municipal de Montjuïc, Montjuïc
Swimming on the slopes

The "Magic Mountain", as it's often called (*see page 89*), shows off plenty of skin in the warmer months as swimmers and sunbathers flock to the waters of its municipal pool. Built in 1929, refurbished for the 1955 Mediterranean Games and expanded for the 1992 Olympics, it attracts professional swimmers, divers and a parade of lithe bodies hoping to work on their tans.

The music video for Kylie Minogue's 2003 synth-pop hit "Slow" was filmed poolside, with the opening shot featuring a toned diver somersaulting into the still waters. Of course, it's a popular spot so we can't guarantee perfect calm – nor Kylie, for that matter.
*31 Avinguda Miramar, 08038
+34 93 423 4041*

Trust me, this is how it's done

③

Piscines Bernat Picornell, Montjuïc
Olympic legacy

One of the best things about hosting the Olympics is being able to make the most of stellar swimming centres afterwards. Located near the Estadi Olímpic Lluís Companys, this complex comprises one indoor and two outdoor pools. Named after the founder of the Spanish Swimming Federation, Bernat Picornell i Richier, it was built in 1970 for the European Aquatics Championships and revamped for the 1992 Olympics. To this day it remains *the* place to do some serious strokes.
*30-38 Avinguda de l'Estadi, 08038
+34 93 423 4041
picornell.cat*

①

**Associació Esportiva Deu Dits,
Bogatell**
Gripping stuff

Bouldering centre Deu Dits
(Catalan for "10 fingers")
has been on the ascent since
opening in 2001. But owners
Joan Giménez i Armengol, Josep
Boixadós i Abella and Lydia
Forest scaled new heights in
2013 when they took over this
space near Poblenou.

The centre opens daily and
is suited to all levels. There's
also a bar and restaurant, as
well as a range of clothing and
equipment. "This is a real
community," says Armengol.
"Anyone is welcome to join."
106 Carrer de Pamplona, 08018
+34 93 624 3699
deudits.com

②

El Ciclo, Barri Gòtic
Peddling pedalling

As pioneers of pedal-powered
travel in the Catalan capital,
the El Ciclo team has gladly
watched Barcelona begin to
take two-wheeled transport
more seriously. The city's
network of bike lanes has
grown exponentially in recent
years, a boon for this fun-
loving firm's expansion.

A standard three-hour tour
sees multilingual leaders delving
into the juicier details of the
city's iconic sites. Alternatively,
rent your own classic model
for a private cycling adventure.
17 Carrer Nou de Sant
Francesc, 08002
+34 93 624 3920
elciclobcn.com

③

**Nike Box Barcelona,
Barceloneta**
Fit for purpose

The sands of Barceloneta may
be suited to athletics but a
lack of proper public facilities
has long been a frustration.
Fortunately sportswear giant
Nike stepped in to fill the void
in 2017, opening its beachside
sports club Box Barcelona.

The first-floor locker space
acts as an open-access meeting
point for anyone practising
yoga, training for a triathlon,
boxing or simply working out
on the sand; an interactive
test in front of a big screen
connects you with teachers
and practitioners. The space
is furnished with the creations
of more than 40 homegrown
designers and hosts artists'
workshops and free concerts.
51 Carrer de Pontevedra, 08003
+34 93 221 4702
nikeboxbarcelona.com

Lap it up

The shopping mall in the
retooled Las Arenas bullfighting
space (*see page 115*) includes
the Metropolitan Gym. A
360-degree alfresco running
track circles the crown of the
structure, while a spa features a
pool, Jacuzzi and Turkish baths.
clubmetropolitan.net

①
Aire Ancient Baths, El Born
Arabic baths

The subterranean caverns of this former 17th-century warehouse once housed ancient wells. Today Aire has repurposed the storied interiors as an Arabic bathing complex that's awash with soothing sounds and smells, and sublime treatments.

Take a preliminary dip in the cool waters of the frigidarium to loosen up any initial tension, then step into the caldarium, a much hotter hammam. End your session with the age-old ritual of a relaxing argan-oil massage.
22 Passeig de Picasso, 08003
+34 93 295 5743
beaire.com

④
Pukas Surf Eskola, Barceloneta
Wave riders

Barcelona is one of the few major European cities where you can catch a decent wave and this surf school's location on Sant Sebastià Beach near Barceloneta adds some serendipity to the swell. Pukas, Spain's most successful surf brand, was founded in the Basque Country in the 1970s by Iñigo Letamendia, his wife Marian Azpiroz and her brother Miguel. It's now in its second generation and has made waves by opening this Catalan branch of the school.

Sharing a location with Club Natació Barcelona – the city's official swim school (*see page 124*) – Pukas caters to everyone, with daily classes and monthly courses for all levels.
93 Passeig de Joan de Borbó, 08039
+34 93 118 6021
pukassurf.com/barcelona

Float your boat

The sensory deprivation tanks at Flotarium are a surefire way to calm the mind and relieve stress: floating in the heavily salted waters is a New Age method of forced meditation. Owner Brendan Cochrane has one recommendation: "Surrender to the silence."
flotarium.com

Grooming greats

01 Peluquería OutCast, Poble-sec: Opened by two rebellious French hairdressers, this salon never shies away from edgier styles.
    +34 93 011 9288

02 Mustache, Dreta de l'Eixample: This old-school barber requires a call ahead to make an appointment: it has but one coveted chair.
    +34 93 002 1942

03 And & S Enobarberia, El Born: A skilled barber who shares his love of fine Italian wine with his clients? This mix of bouffants and booze sits well in the Catalan capital.
    +34 93 001 6992

Beaches
Coasts with the most

Shifting sands

The overcrowded sands of Barceloneta are a little passé. We suggest you take a short trip (just 20 to 30 minutes by train or car) to a more outlying coastal oasis instead.

North of the city you can jog along the flat sands of Montgat, while south are the natural surrounds of El Prat, an antidote to urban beaches, with the popular El Maravillas *chiringuito* (beach bar) providing comfort food for day-trippers. Neighbouring Castelldefels is a more affluent seaside spot and further along the coastline is the fishing village of Garraf, a microcosm of laidback life on the Mediterranean made popular by the restored wooden beach huts perched on the sand.

Running route
Just the jog

① Carretera de les Aigües
Running high

DISTANCE: 9km
GRADIENT: Mainly flat
DIFFICULTY: Moderate
HIGHLIGHT: Forgetting you're in the city
BEST TIME: Weekends
NEAREST MTR: Carretera de les Aigües
(Ferrocarrils de la Generalitat)

Opting for a brisk run along the beach is easy. Anyone looking for a more serious slog should brave the Carretera de les Aigües (Path of the Waters) instead. This 9km-long route derives its name from the archaic water-distribution pipes that once cut through the Serra de Collserola national park. The feat of engineering is now a (mainly) flat running and cycling circuit set among the leafy peaks, with views of the urban sprawl below.

First you'll have to make it up to the elevated starting point. We recommend the 15-minute train ride with the Ferrocarrils service, taking the S1 or S2 lines from Plaça de Catalunya, changing at the Peu del Funicular onto the Vallvidrera line and then disembarking at Carretera de les Aigües. It's less complicated than it sounds – and this spectacular track is worth the trouble.

Cycling route
Pedal power

① Barceloneta
A progressive pedal

DISTANCE: 7km
GRADIENT: Flat
DIFFICULTY: Easy
HIGHLIGHT: Both the coastal breeze and observing the winds of change
BEST TIME: Weekdays
NEAREST MTR: Barceloneta (Line 4)

There's no better way to take in the ongoing urban transformation of Barcelona than by bike. Much of the metamorphosis is visible along the coastline, so what better place to start than on the bustling esplanade of Barceloneta?

As you head north up the designated bike lanes, the hazard posed by absent-minded pedestrians quickly evaporates. Continue up the coastline past the Port Olímpic, admiring the Platja del Bogatell on your right until you reach the futuristic forms of the Parc del Fòrum. Pedalling on you'll reach the Besòs River, where you can join the 5km-long cycle path straddling the riverbank. This path provides an extended view of the successful rehabilitation process that began in 1995, encouraging flora and fauna to flourish along the waterway.

Walks
— Take to the streets

Barcelona is a treat to explore on foot. Whether you're wandering through medieval streets, 19th-century avenues or newly regenerated industrial zones, you'll happen upon peaceful squares, architecture both sparsely modern and riotously baroque, and countless markets, independent shops and galleries. Here we've selected four routes – from buzzy El Raval to peaceful Sant Andreu – that take you away from the usual tourist trail.

El Raval
Urban revival

Once infamous for its artistic denizens, wild cabarets and red-light district, the historic *barri* of El Raval exhibits a certain air of mystery and mischief. But despite the rakish sorts that roamed its gritty alleyways decades ago, the neighbourhood has enjoyed an urban revival in recent years and today is strewn with a plethora of cultural spaces, specialist shops and charming bars, plus one of the city's most popular markets.

Alongside its transformation, El Raval has managed to retain its authentic edge against the tide of mass tourism. There's even a word that encompasses its bon vivant identity: *ravalejar* means leisurely swanning around the neighbourhood, soaking up the atmosphere.

Set off in style
El Raval walk

Hungry for a healthy fix? Look no further than ❶ *Flax & Kale*, a venture from nutritional pioneer Teresa Carles. The contemporary interior may be a sight to behold but don't miss the secluded rooftop garden. After a hearty breakfast (try the pink pitaya bowl) you'll be ready to take in one of Spain's best modern art collections.

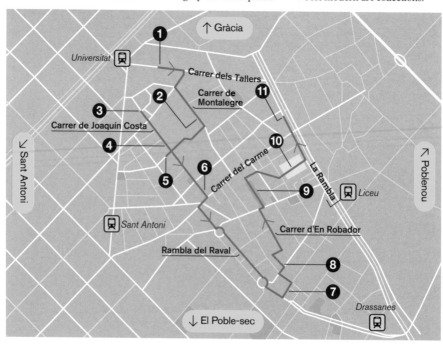

Exit left and take a right turn down Carrer de Valldonzella, followed by a quick left onto Carrer de Montalegre. On Plaça dels Àngels to your right you'll soon see something resembling a colossal white fridge: ❷ *Macba* (*see page 93*). As the modernist structure suggests, the exhibitions often feature striking minimalist and abstract art that can be challenging to grasp but never fails to intrigue.

Stroll across Plaça dels Àngels and take a right turn onto the wonderfully eccentric Carrer de Joaquín Costa, known for its assortment of independent retailers. Start at ❸ *Fusta'm*, one of Barcelona's top vintage furniture shops, full of mid-century gems. Then retrace your steps and continue down the street until you spot ❹ *Les Topettes*, run by young couple Oriol Montañés and Lucia Laurin. Reminiscent of an old pharmacy, it is dedicated to the art of pampering. Try out one of its hand creams then take a right turn at the next corner and enter record shop ❺ *Discos Paradiso*, a delight for vinyl aficionados and a regular host of intimate gigs. End your shopping spree further down Carrer de Joaquín Costa at ❻ *Wilde Vintage Sunglasses*, a cupboard-sized shop with a colossal collection of sunnies dating back to the 1950s.

Make a right turn onto Carrer del Carme and then turn left onto Carrer Maria Aurèlia Capmany, where a roundabout at the end of the street marks the beginning of Rambla del Raval. Strolling down the leafy boulevard leads to an encounter with one of El Raval's most famous residents, Fernando Botero's chubby bronze statue "El Gato" ("The Cat"). At the second roundabout exit onto Carrer de Sant Oleguer then turn left onto Carrer del Marquès de Barberà, where you can

check into ❼ *Trópico* for an exotic brunch. Try the huevos rancheros and the decadent Garden of Delight smoothie.

Exit left and immediately turn left again onto Carrer de Sant Ramon. You'll soon find yourself in front of ❽ *Filmoteca de Catalunya*, a major cultural space boasting an extensive catalogue of arthouse films, as well as ground-floor bar and restaurant La Monroe.

Take yet another left and follow Carrer d'En Robador to the medieval gates of ❾ *Biblioteca de Catalunya*. Originally a hospital – Antoni Gaudí took his last breath here after that fateful tram accident – the building was converted into a library in 1940. Its tranquil courtyard is a welcoming green space among the cobblestones.

Take a shortcut through Plaça de Sant Josep and enter your next stop – ❿ *La Boqueria*, Barcelona's best and busiest food market – from the back. La Boqueria accommodates a rainbow of fruit, vegetables and homemade juices, as well as fish and meat stalls. When you're done exit left onto La Rambla, where a three-minute walk will take you to Hotel 1898 and its inimitable roof terrace ⓫ *La Isabela*, which doubles as a chic cocktail bar. Time it for sunset and you're in for a treat.

Address book

01 Flax & Kale
74B Carrer dels Tallers, 08001
+34 93 317 5664
teresacarles.com/fk

02 Macba
1 Plaça dels Àngels, 08001
+34 93 481 3368
macba.cat

03 Fusta'm
62 Carrer de Joaquín Costa, 08008
+34 639 527 076
fustam.cat

04 Les Topettes
33 Carrer de Joaquín Costa, 08001
+34 93 500 5564
lestopettes.com

05 Discos Paradiso
39 Carrer de Ferlandina, 08001
+34 93 329 6440
discosparadiso.com

06 Wilde Vintage Sunglasses
2 Carrer de Joaquín Costa, 08001
+34 654 455 057
wildesunglasses.com

07 Trópico
24 Carrer del Marquès de Barberà, 08001
+34 93 667 7552
tropicobcn.com

08 Filmoteca de Catalunya
1-9 Plaça de Salvador Seguí, 08001
+34 93 567 1070
filmoteca.cat

09 Biblioteca de Catalunya
56 Carrer de l'Hospital, 08001
+34 93 270 2300
bnc.cat

10 La Boqueria
91 La Rambla, 08001
+34 93 318 2584
boqueria.info

11 La Isabela
109 La Rambla, 08002
+34 93 552 9552
hotel1898.com

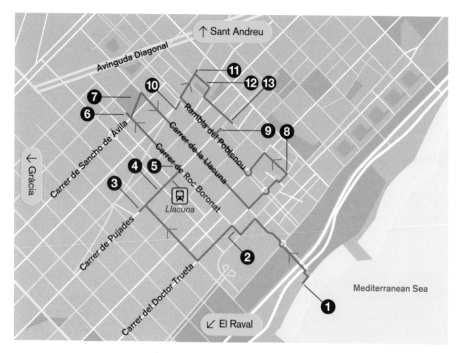

Poblenou
Ex-factory zone

Wide streets, colourful houses from different epochs and a quietly content atmosphere as though it's always Sunday morning: Poblenou feels a world away from the towering blocks of Eixample and the narrow alleys of Ciutat Vella. This *barri* was once the industrial heart of 19th-century Barcelona – it even earned the moniker of the Manchester of Catalonia – but today it's a very different epicentre.

Former factories now house design studios, cultural centres, ateliers, film companies and technology firms (*see page 70*). You'll find these creatives enjoying evening drinks on Rambla del Poblenou – being away from the tourist-trodden centre, life moves a little slower here.

From beach to bars
Poblenou walk

Start with a post-breakfast swim at ❶ *Platja del Bogatell*, a pleasant stretch of urban beach. Then cross the promenade and head northwest on Passatge de la Llacuna. Take a left after the Poblenou cemetery and a right onto Carrer de Roc Boronat, where you'll find Indiana House. This red building is home to Barcelonan brand ❷ *Brava Fabrics*, which makes men's and women's shirts,

T-shirts and swimwear in colourful patterns (*see page 68*).

Exit right and take the first left before heading north on Carrer de Badajoz. After four blocks take another left onto Carrer de Pujades for the best cup of coffee in Barcelona. ❸ *Nømad Roasters' Home* is the work of barista Jordi Mestre, who sources beans from Ethiopia and Guatemala before roasting them here in Poblenou. Once caffeinated, exit left and continue along the street to pick up some old-school vinyl records at prices verging on theft from ❹ *Ultra-Local Records*.

If you'd prefer something more design-minded, continue along the street and take the second left. Here you'll find vintage Scandinavian homeware shop ❺ *Noak Room*. Barcelona has no shortage of great designers but Scandi furniture is a recent addition to the city's design scene and

Address book

01 Platja del Bogatell
80 Paseo Maritimo del
Bogatell, 08005
bcn.cat/platges

02 Brava Fabrics
6 Carrer de Roc Boronat,
08005
+34 65 642 5263
bravafabrics.com

03 Nømad Roasters' Home
95 Carrer de Pujades,
08005
+34 62 856 6235
nomadcoffee.es

04 Ultra-Local Records
113 Carrer de Pujades,
08005
ultralocalrecords.com

05 Noak Room
69 Carrer de Roc Boronat,
08005
+34 93 309 5300
noakroom.com

06 Edificio Media-Tic
117 Carrer de Roc
Boronat, 08018

07 Museu Can Framis
116-126 Carrer de Roc
Boronat, 08018
+34 93 320 8736
fundaciovilacasas.com

08 La Pubilla del Taulat
131 Carrer de Marià
Aguiló, 08005
+34 93 225 3085
lapubilladeltaulat.com

09 Cruixent
173 Carrer de Pujades,
08005
+34 93 105 6047
cruixentbcn.cat

10 Monument to Josep
Trueta
118 Rambla del Poblenou,
08005

11 Sala Beckett
228-232 Carrer de Pere IV,
08005
+34 93 284 5312
salabeckett.cat

12 Espai Subirachs
6 Carrer de Batista, 08005
+34 93 541 5277
subirachs.cat

13 Balius
196 Carrer de Pujades,
08005
+34 93 315 8650
baliusbar.com

Noak Room is firmly at the apex of the movement.

You'll be getting peckish but try to hold out for that late lunch. Continue northwest along Carrer de Roc Boronat until you reach ⑥ *Edificio Media-Tic*. The Rubik's Cube-like structure by Enric Ruiz-Geli is a business and convention centre developed as part of the government-backed 22@Barcelona project, which has been transforming Poblenou into the city's technology-industry hub. It's not all computer processors here though: there's plenty of culture too. To the right is ⑦ *Museu Can Framis*, home to one of the city's main contemporary Catalan art collections. You can also just come to appreciate the building itself: the former textile factory is no less a masterpiece than the canvases within.

Exit the museum and walk southeast down Carrer de la Llacuna. After about 800 metres take a left onto Carrer del Doctor Trueta, traversing the intersecting streets, and follow it onto Carrer de l'Amistat for a traditional lunch at ⑧ *La Pubilla del Taulat*, a no-nonsense tapas bar. It's a place to indulge in the classics: stock up on *pa amb tomàquet*, grilled *padrón* peppers and the house white. Sated and perhaps a tad tipsy, exit right and head north; take the first left and then right onto the tree-lined Rambla del Poblenou, the neighbourhood's main artery. Halfway up on the adjoining Carrer de Pujades is ⑨ *Cruixent*, a bakery serving all things sweet, while a little further along is the fist-like ⑩ *Monument to Josep Trueta* on the central promenade. This statue by sculptor Josep Ricart honours Catalan doctor Josep Trueta, who battled against the Franco regime from exile in the UK during the mid 1900s.

Take the right beyond the monument onto Carrer de Pere IV and you'll soon come to ⑪ *Sala Beckett*, worth exploring for its exquisite interiors. Flores & Prats Architects wonderfully restored the 1920s building, adding modern flourishes while preserving its historic roots.

Around the corner on Carrer de Batista is ⑫ *Espai Subirachs*, a museum dedicated to Josep Maria Subirachs, a sculptor most renowned for his crucifixion scene adorning one of the niches of La Sagrada Família. Exit right from the museum and immediately turn right again, before taking a left onto Carrer de Marià Aguiló and continuing to ⑬ *Balius* (*see page 46*), a retro bar recognisable by its old-school signage. Finish off the afternoon with a well-earned *vermut. Salut i força al canut!*

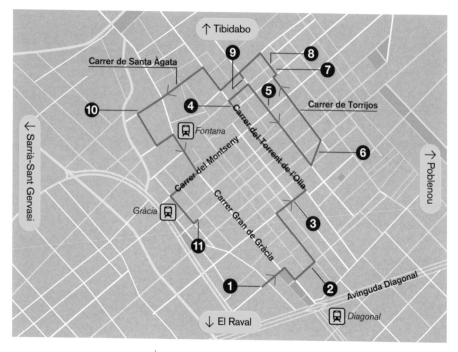

Map labels:
↑ Tibidabo
Carrer de Santa Àgata
← Sarrià-Sant Gervasi
Fontana
Carrer de Torrijos
→ Poblenou
Carrer del Montseny
Carrer del Torrent de l'Olla
Gràcia
Carrer Gran de Gràcia
Avinguda Diagonal
↓ El Raval
Diagonal

Gràcia
Northern light

Gràcia was an independent town until 1897, when it was adopted by Barcelona as the city began to grow outwards. Today it preserves its free roots through lower-rise buildings, annual celebrations during the Festa Major de Gràcia (*see page 79*) and light-filled cafés.

The main hub of this area is the old town, Vila de Gràcia. Perched above the showy Passeig de Gràcia, its narrow tree-lined lanes and picturesque *places* are made for lazy afternoon wanderings. It may not be as twisty as the Barri Gòtic but there are still plenty of opportunities to get lost. Do wander from our path and explore the smaller streets – but here's a concise way to get around and see some of the best of Gràcia in a day.

Quiet lanes and grand squares
Gràcia walk

What better way to sharpen the mind than by beginning your day with a dose of culture at ❶ *Galeria Miquel Alzueta?* Step through the wrought-iron gates into the leafy courtyard just off Carrer de Sèneca and head down the stairs to a former factory space full of art and design that's both contemporary and classic. Next, head back up to the street and continue to the corner where Carrer Gran de Gràcia meets Passeig de Gràcia. Pick up a local newspaper from the kiosk before taking a right and then a left to ❷ *Bar But*, a small café on Carrer de Bonavista, for brunch.

Now to start on the intricate streets. Turn left up the Carrer de Ferrer de Blanes, which quickly turns into the pretty Carrer de Mozart (street

names change rapidly here). Turn right onto Plaça de la Vila de Gràcia, leading to Carrer del Diluvi, and on the corner of Carrer de Martínez de la Rosa you'll find ❸ *The Design Hub Barcelona.* Sustainability is important to the residents

of Gràcia, as you'll gather by the range of design and health shops on offer, and this is one of the best, selling locally designed tableware, lighting and other household objects.

Heading northwest around the corner, continue your shopping trip on Carrer del Torrent de l'Olla. Make sure you look up and take in the contrasting contemporary building of the Biblioteca Vila de Gràcia on the corner of Travessera de Gràcia, designed by Josep Llinás in 2002. Further along you'll find ❹ *8PM*, a modern clothing shop with a contemporary-art gallery attached, boasting clothes and print titles made by Barcelonan designers. Around the corner on Carrer de Verdi you'll see one of the city's best cinemas, Cines Verdi (*see page 104*), or if you want to carry on your shopping spree head to ❺ *The Vos Shop*, which sells fashion from international designers.

As you continue down Carrer de Verdi you'll come to ❻ *Mercat de l'Abaceria*, an undercover market replete with fresh groceries, Spanish condiments and stools to perch on while you refuel. Then again, if it's a sunny day and you're after an alfresco spot, head out of the opposite side of the building and walk back uphill along Carrer de Torrijos.

At the end of the street you'll find Gràcia's best-

looking square, ❼ *Plaça de la Virreina*. Settle in for a drink on the square at Bar Virreina, which tends to get busier with locals as the day goes on, and take in the 19th-century church, Sant Joan Baptista de Gràcia. Once refreshed it's time for a sweet treat. ❽ *Chök* is a Barcelona-based chocolatier that bakes fresh brownies and cakes on site and offers artisanal chocolate bars to take home. As you amble further down the road turn left onto Carrer del Robí, which will take you back to Carrer de Verdi and ❾ *La Festival*. Here you can fill your own bottle of cider from a local selection and browse a large collection of Catalan wines and beers.

Two blocks later hang a right back onto Carrer del Torrent de l'Olla and then take a left onto Carrer de Santa Àgata, which turns into Carrer de les Carolines. Further down the street you'll stumble upon one of Gaudí's masterpieces, ❿ *Casa Vicens*, which only opened to the public in late 2017. With initial construction completed in 1885, this is the first significant design by the architect and it pioneered his work throughout the Catalan capital.

After admiring this landmark take a left down Carrer d'Aulèstia i Pijoan and zigzag down to Plaça de la Llibertat for what will be your final stop: ⓫ *La Pubilla* is a bistro that changes its menu every day depending on the produce available. If it's on offer, polish off your meal with some *crema Catalana*, the burnt custard that Catalonia is famous for. Now that you've successfully navigated Gràcia it will taste even sweeter.

Address book

01 Galeria Miquel Alzueta
9-11 Carrer de Sèneca, 08006
+34 93 238 9750
galeriamiquelalzueta.net

02 Bar But
8 Carrer de Bonavista, 08012
+34 93 360 7128
barbut.es

03 The Design Hub Barcelona
53 Carrer de Martínez de la Rosa, 08012
+34 93 315 4695

04 8PM
164 Carrer del Torrent de l'Olla, 08012
+34 93 012 9155
8pmstore.com

05 The Vos Shop
24 Carrer de Verdi, 08012
+34 93 311 2114
thevosshop.com

06 Mercat de l'Abaceria
186 Travessera de Gràcia, 08012
+34 93 213 6286
mercatabaceria.com

07 Plaça de la Virreina
Plaça de la Virreina, 08024

08 Chök
93 Carrer d'Astúries, 08024
+34 93 348 7616
chokbarcelona.com

09 La Festival
67 Carrer de Verdi, 08012
+34 93 023 2281

10 Casa Vicens
20-26 Carrer de les Carolines, 08012
+34 93 547 5980
casavicens.org

11 La Pubilla
23 Plaça de la Llibertat, 08012
+34 93 218 2994

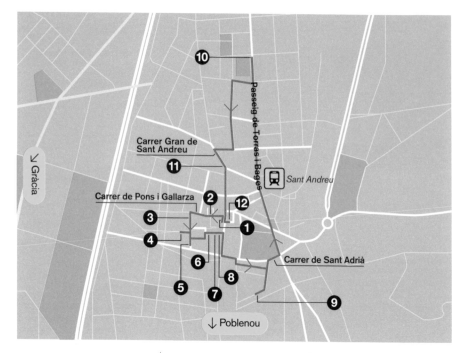

Sant Andreu
Keeping it real

A small-town pace persists in this much quieter corner of the city. It's one of the first clues to Sant Andreu's storied heritage as a separate settlement turned industrial hotbed and ultimately part of metropolitan Barcelona when it was annexed in 1897.

Also known as District 9 (though nothing like Neill Blomkamp's dystopian thriller), Barcelona's most outlying *barri* is an area where a steely working class has banded together across generations to reinvent its future. If you're looking to soak up a more authentic neighbourhood atmosphere, Sant Andreu feels a world away from the perpetual stream of tourists parading up and down La Rambla.

Walk on the quiet side
Sant Andreu walk

It makes sense to start at the Sant Andreu metro stop in Plaça d'Orfila, just a 20-minute ride from the city centre. Head past the Seu del Districte building and along the thoroughfare of Carrer de l'Ajuntament until you reach the Plaça del Comerç. Looming in front of you, the turquoise-green Casa Vidal is a bright example of *modernista* architecture. Spot the decorative mosaics known as *trencadís* and the beloved ground-level ❶ *Bar Versalles*. Its basement was once used as a bunker during the civil war but today the statuesque female-figured lamps help elderly men read the daily newspapers. An elevated rear dining hall serves dishes such as *callos a la catalana* (Catalan tripe) and *entrecot de Girona* (Girona-style steak).

After getting your fill, head up Carrer de Pons i Gallarza, past the politically charged graffiti reflecting the area's combative spirit, and stop at ❷ *Dibarcafé General Store* for a freshly roasted coffee accompanied by an *ensaïmada* (Mallorcan pastry). Continuing up the same street, notice the two-storey cottages built for the railway and factory workers who are said to have planted the *naranjos* (orange trees) that give these streets their aromatic ambience.

Turn left at Carrer de Vintró – dropping by ❸ *3Dealo*, a 3D printing studio helmed by a duo of enterprising Brazilians – and continue through the stone archway into the market square. The Mercat de Sant Andreu has withstood the test of time (and modernity) and is still surrounded by family-owned businesses. Sample traditional Catalan *carquinyolis* (biscotti) and

Address book

01 **Bar Versalles**
255 Carrer Gran de Sant
Andreu, 08030
+34 93 179 4907
barversalles.cat

02 **Dibarcafé General Store**
9-13 Carrer de Pons i
Gallarza, 08030
+34 93 346 8800
dibarcafe.com

03 **3Dealo**
3 Carrer de Vintró, 08030
+34 93 138 9374
3dealo.com

04 **Pastisseria Ribalta**
19 Plaça del Mercadal,
08030
+34 93 345 0877

05 **Formatgeria Subirana**
15 Plaça del Mercadal,
08030
+34 93 345 7239

06 **Rabasseda**
1 Plaça del Mercadal,
08030
+34 67 753 7803

07 **Futurniture**
5 Carrer del Mercat,
08030
+34 661 864 546
futurniture.es

08 **Frankfurt's**
231 Carrer Gran de Sant
Andreu, 08030
+34 93 140 1829

09 **Fabra i Coats**
20 Carrer de Sant Adrià,
08030
+34 93 256 6150
fabraicoats.bcn.cat

10 **Casa Bloc**
95-101 Passeig de Torras
i Bages, 08030
+34 93 256 6801
*museudeldisseny.
barcelona.cat*

11 **Farmàcia Guinart**
306 Carrer Gran de Sant
Andreu, 08030
+34 93 345 0307
farmaciaguinart.com

12 **Farmàcia Franquesa**
260 Carrer Gran de Sant
Andreu, 08030
+34 93 345 2341

panellets (cookies eaten on All Saints' Day) at the third-generation ❹ *Pastisseria Ribalta* or marvel at the mouth-watering selection of farmers' cheeses at ❺ *Formatgeria Subirana*. Plus, enjoy a glass of wine and a hearty dish cooked with market-fresh ingredients at the much-loved ❻ *Rabasseda* bar and restaurant.

Walking past the latter's wonderfully retro tiled wall and along Carrer del Mercat you'll notice ❼ *Futurniture* on your right, a colourful repository of vintage design and modern ornaments. Before turning right down Carrer Gran de Sant Andreu, poke your nose into ❽ *Frankfurt's*, a German-themed bar with decor that feels frozen in the 1960s. Continue along the neighbourhood's main street and turn left down Carrer de Sant Adrià, through the verdant square and past the modern market building on your right, until you reach the former ❾ *Fabra i Coats* industrial complex. This is the district's beating cultural heart, hosting a contemporary-art gallery, concert hall and even a *castells* (human castle) school for kids.

Follow Carrer del Segre past the neoclassical cathedral until you reach ❿ *Casa Bloc*. Designed and built by a group of progressive architects during Spain's Second Republic in the 1930s, it's an outstanding monument to early rationalism (*see page 114*); guided tours provide a more privileged peek inside each Saturday. The stilted S-shaped structure allows you to cross diagonally beneath it onto Carrer de Lanzarote, turning right down Carrer Guardiola i Feliu and back onto Carrer Gran de Sant Andreu. Veer left and you'll soon spot the original wood-and-ceramic façade of ⓫ *Farmàcia Guinart*, which has been attending to residents' ailments since 1896.

Continue straight and you'll unexpectedly arrive back in Plaça del Comerç, where another chemist – ⓬ *Farmàcia Franquesa*, built in 1842 – installed its antique interiors into a more modern apartment building that rose up in its place. With your tour through Sant Andreu's layered history complete, head back to the city centre on the metro, where a more frenetic world awaits.

Resources
— Inside knowledge

We've shown you where to source the freshest seafood, pointed out the plushest places to stay and rounded up some first-rate retail offerings. We've combed the gridded streets for the most cutting-edge commercial galleries and, naturally, drawn up a lengthy list of architectural feats designed by Gaudí.

Now all you need are some fast facts and top tips for navigating the city, from hailing a taxi to bagging a seat on the bus. Check out the events taking place while you're in town and make a note of what to do if the heavens open. Plus, discover a bunch of Barcelona tunes and learn a little Catalan to impress the locals.

Transport
Getting around

01 Metro: Barcelona's metro – composed of eight main lines – is tidy, speedy and very rarely crowded. A single ticket will set you back €2.20 but we recommend the T-10: this 10-journey ticket can be used by multiple people and costs a reasonable €9.95. *tmb.cat*

02 Bus: Walking around Barcelona is a pleasant pastime but if you need a boost, jump on a bus; be sure to buy a ticket from the metro station first. Certain tickets are valid on both buses and metro. *tmb.cat*

03 Taxi: Taxis are plentiful in the city and easily spotted by their black-and-yellow livery. All journeys have a base charge of €2.10, with an additional €1.10 or so per kilometre. Keep in mind that drivers charge a €1 supplement for any suitcases. *taxi.amb.cat*

04 Funicular: Montjuïc is a fair hike so hitch a ride on the funicular if you're not feeling up for the trek. It costs €2.15 and takes you from Carrer Nou de la Rambla in Poble-sec to Avinguda Miramar near Fundació Joan Miró (*see pages 97 and 118*), where it links up with the *telefèric* (cable car) that whizzes up to Montjuïc Castle. The latter may be more pricey, at €12.70, but it's worth it for the sweeping views over the city. *tmb.cat*

Airports
Runway success

01 Barcelona-El Prat Airport: The city's main airport revamp by architect Ricardo Bofill was unveiled in 2009. With the gleaming updated look came a super transport system: it's fast, cheap and efficient. Hop on line L9S for €4.50 and change at Torrassa to get to the city centre. Otherwise you can jump in one of the many cabs neatly stationed outside the terminal gates for €25 to €30. *aena.es*

Vocabulary
Local lingo

Català, or Catalan, is the lingua franca of Catalonia. And it's not a dialect of Spanish but rather a Romance language of its own (it's also the official language of Andorra). Spanish will get you by just fine but to get in a Barcelonan's good books, learn a few Catalan expressions.

01 Adéu: Bye
02 Barri: Neighbourhood
03 Bon dia a tothom: Hello everybody
04 Com estem bon amic? How are you, old chum?
05 De res: You're welcome
06 Molt de gust: Pleasure to meet you
07 Moltes mercès: Thank you
08 Pa amb tomàquet: Bread topped with tomatoes and olive oil
09 Perdoni: Excuse me/sorry
10 Si us plau: Please

Soundtrack to the city
Top tunes

01 **'Clandestino' by Manu Chao:** Paris-born Manu Chao has long lived in Barcelona and *Clandestino*, mainly performed in Spanish, is perhaps his most famous album. The title track is all about immigration.

02 **'La Revolución Sexual' by La Casa Azul:** Formed in the late 1990s, La Casa Azul blurs the lines between J-pop and Europop. Its disco track "La Revolución Sexual" was entered into the bid for the 2008 Eurovision Song Contest but was, sadly, pipped at the post.

03 **'Young' by Pavvla:** Folk-pop singer Pavvla released her debut album *Creatures* with Luup records. Reminiscent of Lana Del Rey, Pavvla is a good starting point to explore the back catalogue of this Barcelona-based record label that's the home of plenty more local acts.

04 **'Un Sentimiento Importante' by Mujeres:** Barcelona loves a good rock concert and native guitar band Mujeres caters for that craving. The trio play jangly garage tunes that will keep your toes tapping late into the evening.

05 **'Barcelona' by Freddie Mercury and Montserrat Caballé:** How could we not include the most famous song ever written about Barcelona? This 1987 duet between the Queen frontman and Barcelonan opera singer became the song of the 1992 Summer Olympics in the Catalan capital.

Best events
What to see

01 **La Calçotada:** *Calçots* (leek-like onions) are grilled on open fires across Catalonia. *February to March*

02 **080 Barcelona Fashion:** Becoming a prominent event on the global catwalk calendar. *January/February and June/July, 080barcelonafashion.cat*

03 **Barcelona Carnival:** A week of exotic dancers, enormous effigies and plentiful parades. *February*

04 **Festa de Sant Medir:** Sweets and chocolates are dished out in Gràcia. *3 March*

05 **Diada de Sant Jordi:** Like Valentine's Day, except boys give girls a rose and girls give boys a book. *23 April*

06 **Primavera Sound:** Some 200,000 people descend on Parc del Fòrum for a few days of live music. *May to June, primaverasound.es*

07 **Sónar:** This three-day electro festival has been running since 1994. *June, sonar.es*

08 **Nit de Sant Joan:** The summer solstice features fireworks, street parties and fruit-laden pastries called *coca de Sant Joan*. *23-24 June*

09 **Festa Major de Gràcia:** A celebration that culminates with an enormous alfresco dinner (*see page 79*). *15-21 August, festamajordegracia.cat*

10 **La Mercè:** Come see the *sardana* (a traditional Catalan dance) and *castells* (human towers). *22-25 September*

Sunny days
The great outdoors

01 **Tibidabo Mountain:** For stunning views and respite from the city, head to the mountain-top Sagrat Cor church, a 20-minute drive to the north.

02 **Montjuïc:** Wander around the grounds of Montjuïc Castle, enjoy a picnic under the trees and drop by the various museums dotting the slopes, including the Fundació Joan Miró.

03 **Beach:** If Barceloneta is too crowded head to Bogatell or Mar Bella, two cleaner strips of sand further up the coast. If you see the lifeguard raise a yellow flag, beware: there are jellyfish in the water.

Rainy days
Weather-proof activities

01 **Palau de la Música Catalana:** Duck under the safety of the concert hall's stained-glass dome and let the sweet sounds of Tárrega and Granados carry you away. *palaumusica.cat*

02 **Churros:** Take your time over an enormous, sugary churro and cup of rich hot chocolate at Churrería Laietana or Granja M Viader as you watch the rain pitter-patter.

03 **L'Aquarium Barcelona:** The aquarium boasts an impressive underwater walkway that gets you up close and personal with hundreds of different species. *aquariumbcn.com*

About Monocle
——— Step inside

In 2007, Monocle was launched as a monthly magazine briefing on global affairs, business, culture, design and much more. We believed there was a globally minded audience of readers who were hungry for opportunities and experiences beyond their national borders.

Today Monocle is a complete media brand with print, audio and online elements – not to mention our expanding network of shops and cafés. Besides our London HQ we have six international bureaux in New York, Toronto, Singapore, Tokyo, Zürich and Hong Kong. We continue to grow and flourish and at our core is the simple belief that there will always be a place for a print brand that is committed to telling fresh stories and sending photographers on assignments. It's also a case of knowing that our success is all down to the readers, advertisers and collaborators who have supported us along the way.

London HQ
———
Our editorial office is in Marylebone

❶
International bureaux
Boots on the ground

We have a headquarters in London and call upon firsthand reports from our contributors in more than 35 cities around the world. We also have six international bureaux. For this travel guide, MONOCLE reporters Melkon Charchoglyan and Holly Fisher decamped to Barcelona to explore all that it has to offer. They also called on various contacts, including our Madrid correspondent Liam Aldous, to ensure that we have covered the best in retail, hospitality, culture and more.

❷
Online
Digital delivery

We have a dynamic website: *monocle.com*. As well as being the place to hear our radio station, Monocle 24, the site presents our films, which are beautifully shot and edited by our in-house team and provide a fresh perspective on our stories. Check out the films celebrating the cities that make up our Travel Guide Series before you explore the rest of the site.

❸
Retail and cafés
Food for thought

Via our shops in Hong Kong, Toronto, New York, Tokyo, London and Singapore we sell products that cater to our readers' tastes and are produced in collaboration with brands we believe in. We also have cafés in Tokyo and London. And if you are in the UK capital visit the Kioskafé in Paddington, which combines good coffee and great reads.

❹
Print
Committed to the page

MONOCLE is published 10 times a year. We also produce two standalone publications – THE FORECAST, packed with insights into the year ahead, and THE ESCAPIST, our summer travel-minded magazine – and seasonal weekly newspapers. Since 2013 we have also been publishing books, like this one, in partnership with Gestalten. Visit *monocle.com/subscribe*.

❺
Radio
Sound approach

Monocle 24 is our round-the-clock radio station that was launched in 2011. It delivers global news and shows covering foreign affairs, urbanism, business, culture, food and drink, design and print media. When you find yourself in Barcelona, tune into *The Globalist* for a newsy start to your morning. You can listen live or download any of our shows from *monocle.com*, iTunes or SoundCloud.

Priority service
—
Subscribers save 10 per cent in our online shop

Join the club

01
Subscribe to Monocle
A subscription is a simple way to make sure that you never miss an issue – and you'll enjoy many additional benefits.

02
Be in the know
Our subscribers have exclusive access to the entire Monocle archive, and priority access to selected product collaborations, at *monocle.com*.

03
Stay in the loop
Subscription copies are delivered to your door at no extra cost no matter where you are in the world. We also offer an auto-renewal service to ensure that you never miss an issue.

04
And there's more...
Subscribers benefit from a 10 per cent discount at all Monocle shops, including online, and receive exclusive offers and invitations to events around the world.

Choose your package

Premium one year
12 × issues
+ Porter Sub Club bag

One year
12 × issues
+ Monocle Voyage tote bag

Six months
6 × issues

Chief photographer
Silvia Conde

Photographer
Salva López

Writers
Liam Aldous
Inma Buendía
Melkon Charchoglyan
Eloise Edgington
Josh Fehnert
Holly Fisher
Begoña Gómez Urzaiz
Katie Jennings
Julia Keller
Anette Lien
Raphael Minder
Inés Miró-Sans
Marta Puigdemasa
Carlos Román Alcaide
Jolyon Sayer
Saul Taylor
Sam Zucker

Still life
David Sykes

Images
Alamy
Nacho Alegre
Metrixell Arjalaguer
Xavier Padrós
Olga Planas
Aniol Resclosa
Soho House Barcelona
Pol Viladoms

Illustrators
Satoshi Hashimoto
Ceylan Sahin
Tokuma

Monocle
EDITOR IN CHIEF AND
CHAIRMAN
Tyler Brûlé
EDITOR
Andrew Tuck
CREATIVE DIRECTOR
Richard Spencer Powell

CHAPTER EDITING

Need to know
Saul Taylor

Hotels
Josh Fehnert

Food and drink
Sam Zucker

Retail
Liam Aldous

Things we'd buy
Melkon Charchoglyan

Essays
Melkon Charchoglyan
Joe Pickard

Culture
Holly Fisher

Design and architecture
Melkon Charchoglyan

Sport and fitness
Liam Aldous

Walks
Melkon Charchoglyan

Resources
Melkon Charchoglyan

**The Monocle Travel Guide
Series: Barcelona**
GUIDE EDITOR
Melkon Charchoglyan
ASSOCIATE GUIDE EDITORS
Liam Aldous
Holly Fisher
PHOTO EDITOR
Victoria Cagol

**The Monocle Travel Guide
Series**
SERIES EDITOR
Joe Pickard
ASSOCIATE EDITOR
Chloë Ashby
ASSISTANT EDITOR
Mikaela Aitken
WRITER
Melkon Charchoglyan
DESIGNER
Loi Xuan Ly
PHOTO EDITORS
Matthew Beaman
Shin Miura
Victoria Cagol

PRODUCTION
Jacqueline Deacon
Dan Poole
Rachel Kurzfield
Sean McGeady
Sonia Zhuravlyova

Research
Sophia Ahmadi
Dan Einav
Will Kitchens
Natasha Kleeman
Katherine Mendoza Malagon
Paige Reynolds
Aliz Tennant
Katie Waktins

Special thanks
Milly Baker
Doïna Becker
Pauline den Hartog Jager
Adrien Harrison
Llucià Homs
Helena Kardová
Lewis Kopman
Mari Luz Vidal
Museu Picasso
Kate Sinclair
Andrew Trotter

New

The collection

Planning another trip? We have a global suite of guides, with many more set to be released in the coming months. Cities are fun. Let's explore.

Buy today at all good bookshops

You can also visit the online shops at *monocle.com* and *shop.gestalten.com* to get hold of your copies.

Right, where next?